SPORTS FOR YOUR CHILD

SPORTS FOR YOUR CHILD

George Sullivan

Winchester Press

Library of Congress Catalog Card No. 73–78828
ISBN 0–87691–120–3

Published by Winchester Press
460 Park Avenue, New York 10022

Printed in the United States of America

CONTENTS

Introduction   1

I Racket Sports

TENNIS   7
BADMINTON   16
TABLE TENNIS   21
OTHER COURT GAMES   28

II Individual Sports

GOLF   33
SKIING   44
RIDING   55
ICE SKATING   59

FENCING   66

BOWLING   70

ARCHERY   77

III   Aquatic Sports

SWIMMING AND DIVING   89

SNORKEL DIVING AND SCUBA DIVING   98

WATER SKIING   111

IV   Shooting Sports

RIFLERY   121

SHOTGUNNING   131

V   Outdoor Activities

BOATING   143

SAILING   150

CANOEING   156

BACKPACKING   162

FISHING   175

BICYCLING   182

VI   Combative Sports

WRESTLING   197

BOXING   203

JUDO AND KARATE   206

VII Team Sports

TEAM SPORTS IN GENERAL   215

BASEBALL   222

FOOTBALL   229

BASKETBALL   235

SOCCER   240

SOFTBALL   247

ICE HOCKEY   251

VOLLEYBALL   258

GYMNASTICS   261

TRACK AND FIELD   266

Photograph Credits   274

SPORTS
FOR
YOUR
CHILD

INTRODUCTION

Fun.

That's what children want from sports.

Fun means excitement, the thrill of diving from the high board or streaking in from third base on an infield hit. Fun means being with one's friends, maybe a game of volleyball at the beach or bowling after school. Fun is being part of a team.

Fun also means the satisfaction that comes from doing something very well, better than almost anyone. And the recognition that follows.

This book is meant to help you, as a parent, select a sport for your child. Fun—your child's fun—should be the main consideration. But you should also encourage your child to take up a sport that will provide for his physical well-being.

Americans, young and old, are devoting less and less of their time to activities that require vigorous physical exertion. The operative word is *vigorous*. It implies sweating and breathing hard. Only by *vigorous* exercise can a person attain fitness, and being fit means leading a healthier, happier and more zestful life.

So by the time your son or daughter is age ten or so, you should begin encouraging an interest in a sport that has some health-giving benefits. As Dr. Kenneth Cooper says in his book *Aerobics,* "These are very critical years, when his young body is filling out, and should be the years when he gets his heart and lungs in shape for their life's work.''

In recent years, medical experts have come to equate fitness with the health of the lungs and the entire cardiovascular system. Fitness should be measured, they say, in terms of oxygen consumption, the amount of oxygen the body can bring in and deliver to the energy-producing organs and tissues.

The most efficient activities for developing high oxygen consumption are running, swimming and cycling, and so sports that involve these activities to a significant degree—as, for example, basketball, soccer, handball, tennis, and track and field events all involve running—rate high as healthy exercise.

Major American sports such as baseball and football don't rate very well. As stop-and-go sports, they fail to make sufficient demands on the body's oxygen-producing system. Even golf doesn't get good grades. Four hours of trodding a course does impart some physical benefits, of course, but the sport can't be considered what Dr. Cooper would term a ''basic conditioner.''

Calisthenics and isometrics are limited in value, too. They're excellent for developing the skeletal muscles, but a person's muscles can bulge and he can still be lacking in physical fitness.

Most of the sports and activities related to running, swimming and cycling are also valuable because they have a carry-over aspect: they can be played for one's entire lifetime. After graduation from high school, where is the football player going to find twenty-one other boys to play football? Where is the shortstop going to find seventeen other baseball players? In college, maybe. But after college, where?

The psychological benefits to be derived from sports must be considered too. Boys and girls, especially adolescents, need to feel accepted, and their desire for recognition is strong. Sports can play a role in this respect. They help to develop a youngster's initiative and self-confidence.

To some degree, the structure of a child's body is going to dictate the sports for which he is best suited. From the earliest, a child manifests specific structural characteristics, and year by year they become more pronounced.

Some children have bodies which are vaguely square in shape. They have thick necks and their legs, arms and fingers are short. Their hands and feet are small in proportion to the rest of their body. A child with these bodily characteristics usually has the size, strength and

Introduction

stamina to play contact sports. He may lack in speed and quickness, however.

Other children have wide shoulders and narrow hips. And while they have a bony framework, they are merely lean, not thin. They have muscles that are firm and powerful but do not bulge. Youngsters with these characteristics have the physical potential to do well in almost any sport.

Still other children are tall and slender, with thin legs, arms and fingers. They have small muscles and narrow shoulders. Youngsters of this type are obviously not well suited for contact sports, but there are many sports in which they can excel—basketball, the racket sports, and track events such as sprints and jumps.

It must be said at once that no child manifests these traits in a pure form. But each tends toward one of them. You can tell whether your child is going to be a defensive tackle or javelin thrower at a very early age.

There are some sports that you yourself can teach to your child, like swimming, ice skating and sailing. With others, like fencing and riding, you will have to rely on a professional instructor. But either way, you should understand what is involved in learning a sport. If you are teaching what are sometimes called "motor skills," there are certain techniques that you should follow.

The first step is always to explain the movement; the second is to demonstrate it. Then let your youngster do it and correct any mistakes in his form. Whether it's springboard diving or marble-shooting, youngsters learn by doing.

In other words, a learner teaches himself. Your role as an instructor is chiefly to help him to eliminate his errors.

This theory of instruction takes advantage of the fact that children are natural mimics. If you happen to be a good skier, you get a child to master the sport's fundamentals by having him play follow-the-leader with you. The child may not have the vaguest idea of what "counter motion" or "counter rotation" or similar technical terms mean, yet by following you down a gentle slope he will be able to execute moves that utilize these principles.

It's also important to realize that each child learns in his own way and at his own rate of speed. If you're instructing two or more youngsters at the same time, don't expect the same progress from each.

Practicing is vital, of course, but it's only of value if the youngster has learned the correct form; otherwise it can be detrimental.

Tailor the amount of practice to the youngster's span of interest and fatigue level. Generally, frequent short periods of practice are superior to infrequent and extended ones.

Books and booklets, and visual aids like films and film strips, enhance the child's learning process. But these are to be considered secondary to demonstrating a motion and then having the child execute it. Make him perform.

The best way to teach the rules of a game is by explaining them in relation to the skill involved. For example, you should show a youngster where to stand in serving a tennis ball and explain where the ball must be placed at the same time you teach the serving stroke. Be sure to point out the reason behind each rule. Never bend a rule for a youngster. Doing so usually serves to diminish his sense of achievement.

Your local library or neighborhood bookstore is likely to have available instruction textbooks on just about any sport you can name. You can also order instruction manuals by mail. The Sports Illustrated Library consists of books containing instruction information on virtually all popular sports. Priced at $3.95 each, they can be ordered from J. B. Lippincott Company (E. Washington Sq., Philadelphia, Penna. 19105).

The Athletic Institute (Room 705, Merchandise Mart, Chicago, Ill. 60654), a nonprofit organization devoted to the advancement of physical education and recreation, has compiled a comprehensive library of instruction booklets, each about 60 pages in length and costing $1. Each contains sequence pictures which demonstrate correct form. Write for a listing of titles.

A final word: Be certain your child *wants* to learn before you begin any instruction program. Forcing a sport on him can only lead to disappointment, for both your youngster and yourself.

I   RACKET SPORTS

TENNIS
BADMINTON
TABLE TENNIS
OTHER COURT GAMES

TENNIS

There are more than a few physical fitness experts and high school athletic coaches who will tell you that tennis is the best sport there is for a growing boy or girl. I do not dispute them.

Tennis is vigorous exercise. During the normal five-set match, the average player runs well over two miles at sprinting speed. Tennis demands not only speed of foot and stamina, but power and accuracy as well. However, a player who lacks in any one of these qualities can make up for it by being strong in the others.

Tennis is also valuable because it teaches self-reliance. At least in singles, when a player loses he has no one to blame but himself. The game's emphasis on court manners helps to teach courtesy. Finally, tennis has social values. From the first day your child takes it up, he'll be brought into contact with boys and girls of all ages.

At what age can you begin teaching a child tennis? George Seewagen, a former president of the U.S. Professional Tennis Association and one of the most respected instructors in the Northeast, recalls that he and his wife began teaching their two youngsters, a boy and a girl, the fundamentals of the sport as infants, even before the children were walking. "We began," says Seewagen, "by taking a balloon and tossing it toward the child as he lay in the crib. And the baby would hit it back. This taught hand-eye coordination—and the kids loved it.

"Later, when the children reached the toddling stage, we'd set up an indoor 'court' on the living-room coffee table, and we'd station one of the youngsters at one end. A row of books served as a net. The child and I would hit a balloon back and forth.

"As the children became older, we'd bounce a tennis ball to them and they'd hit it back with an open hand. We always encouraged them to use an overhand stroke, like the stroke in tennis."

However, Eve Kraft, co-chairman of the U.S. Lawn Tennis Association's Education and Research Committee, recommends that parents wait until a child has entered the third or fourth grade before beginning tennis instruction. "Cases can be cited where success was obtained at an earlier age," she says, "but usually a child's motor, mental and emotional maturity have not sufficiently developed to be able to handle the complicated skills and rules of tennis before eight or nine years of age."

The particular style of play a child develops should be tailored to his physical strengths or weaknesses. If a youngster can't cope with the volley, there's no use having him rush the net. And if he has height and good reach, you don't want him scampering all over the court; let him overpower his opponents.

A child's style will also come to be an extension of his or her temperament. Of course, this is true in every sport. Joe Namath doesn't run the New York Jets the way Bob Griese runs the Miami Dolphins. You're not going to keep a youngster who is naturally eager and impatient at the baseline hitting ground strokes.

It follows that a young player should not necessarily emulate a tennis star. Your daughter might watch Chris Evert and decide, "Chrissie likes to stay in the backcourt and hit groundstrokes. That's what I'm going to do." It might be a wise decision; it also might not be.

Tennis players—indeed, participants in any of the racket sports—are extremely conscious of left-handedness. When a left-hander hits, the ball leaves the racket with the "wrong" spin. It used to be that left-handers were looked upon as if they were afflicted in some way, and coaches would try to change them. Not any more. If your youngster is a leftie, so be it. It's not just that educational theories have changed. Another reason is a leftie by the name of Rod Laver.

TENNIS EQUIPMENT

Tennis has undergone some significant changes in recent years, with the introduction of new scoring systems, synthetic playing surfaces and open tournaments. Another is the metal racket—tubular steel, aluminum or magnesium.

Metal rackets are half an inch shorter than the wood models and have open shafts to cut down wind resistance, making for a faster, more powerful stroke. The user also gets added punch because the head design is round rather than oval, like wood rackets, and this gives greater tension in the string area. These factors may not mean a great deal until the youngster has advanced beyond the novice stage. But even the untried beginner will benefit from one other advantage that metal rackets offer, and that is durability. Metal will withstand the wear and tear even on asphalt courts.

Of the three types of metal rackets, magnesium is the most expensive, costing about $50. Make your choice between steel and aluminum. Prices begin at $20, unstrung, and ascend to about $40.

Right after metal rackets were introduced in the late 1960s, they enjoyed a great surge of popularity and manufacturers were unable to keep up with the demand. Then followed a leveling-off period. In recent years, there has been something of a trend back to wood—laminated wood, of course. Buy a wood racket for a youngster whose game features control rather than power. Some players claim that a wood racket enables a player to "feel closer to the ball." Expect to pay $20 to $30 for a quality wood racket.

Just as important as the choice between metal or wood is the matter of racket weight and size. Rackets range in weight from 11½ ounces, which might be suitable for a young, slightly built beginner, to 14½ ounces, which would be appropriate for an experienced adult player. Discourage the idea that the heavier the racket, the more power the young player will be able to muster. Power relates much more to timing and coordination than to racket weight. Evidence of this is the fact that Pancho Gonzales, in the later stages of his career, used a racket that weighed only 13 ounces.

All of these figures are "strung weights." If you buy an unstrung racket, allow ¾ ounce for stringing material.

As far as the kind of string is concerned, you have a choice between nylon or lamb gut (not catgut). For young players nylon is better because it lasts longer and is less expensive. The cost of stringing with nylon runs from $6 to $12 for wood rackets, $8 to $17 for metal. Gut stringing is several dollars more in each case.

Have the youngster's instructor or the club pro advise you as to the amount of tension the racket string should have. He will probably recommend 55 to 60 pounds.

Be sure your child's hand fits comfortably about the racket handle. Handles range in circumference (in gradations of ⅛ inch) from 4¼ to 5 inches.

Really young players, not being able to grasp the racket as firmly as an adult, are often bothered by handle slipperiness on hot and humid days. There are a couple of things you can do to cope with the problem. One is to have the grip leather reversed (in a tennis shop), so the rough side is outside. Or you can cover the handle with a terrycloth grip. These are self-sticking and wrap around the handle.

Once your young player is out of the novice stage, don't be surprised if he asks for a second racket. More and more young players want two. One may be metal, the other wood, or one strung with nylon and the other gut. Or the player may want a variation in the racket weight or handle size. During competition he will switch from one to the other, depending on conditions.

Just as metal rackets have taken precedence over those of wood, so leather tennis shoes have supplanted those of canvas. Leather sneakers are lighter, they last longer, and their perforated uppers provide the feet with welcome ventilation. Adidas, a German company noted for its track shoes, pioneered in the development of leather shoes for tennis, but many firms now have them available. A pair costs $15 to $18.

Tennis balls cost $2 to $3 for three. If your child plays on clay, concrete or asphalt, buy the pressureless ball, which gets its bounce from its elasticized superstructure. Balls of this type last much longer than the conventional ball. Punch a hole in one and it will continue to bounce. They can be cleaned in a washing machine. They cost about the same as pressurized balls.

10

INSTRUCTION FOR JUNIORS

Probably the biggest problem that instructors have in teaching young children to play tennis is dealing with their lack of concentration. It's not a *complete* lack, of course; it's just that a child's attention span is shorter than an adult's. There is little you can do about this. If a child is determined to learn the game, to excel, then you have no real worry. If he's indifferent . . . well, perhaps some other sport would be better.

There are usually fewer problems in teaching the sport's techniques—the strokes and the footwork. If the instructor demonstrates how to grip the racket and how to execute a forehand stroke, and then says to the child, "Do it like this," the child, in most cases, will. When it comes to imitating another person's physical actions, most children have a natural aptitude.

To select an instructor for your child, perhaps the best place to begin is the Yellow Pages of your telephone directory. Check the listings under the heading "Tennis Instruction."

Find out as much about the course as you can before you enroll your child. Is the instruction private or group? If it's group instruction, how many youngsters make up a class? (More than eight is unwieldy.) There's nothing wrong with group instruction—in fact, most youngsters prefer this type. For eight to ten one-hour group lessons, the cost should range from $60 to $75. Private lessons from resident pros vary from $10 to $30 an hour.

America's most successful tennis teacher of recent years has to be Jim Evert, instructor at the Holiday Tennis Center in Fort Lauderdale, Florida. Evert gives lessons about four hours a day to the general

public, then spends time with his youngsters. These include Chris, the star of the family, at seventeen the No. 1 ranking woman amateur, and rated No. 3 by the USLTA behind Billie Jean King and Nancy Richey Gunter; Jeanne, fourteen, ranked No. 1 nationally among girls fourteen and under; John, ten, rated No. 9 in Florida in the twelve-and-under age group; and Clare, four, who hits tennis balls using a sawed-off racket, a "fly-swatter" as her father calls it.

Jim Evert didn't set out with the idea of developing a family of champions. Because he didn't want to be separated from his family on weekends, his busiest time as a tennis pro, Evert asked his wife to start bringing the youngsters over to the courts. One by one, as they reached the age of five, he had them start hitting balls against a cement wall. When he saw they had some talent, he began giving them lessons.

As the youngsters improved, Evert set down a rigorous schedule for each. It included two hours of practice at Holiday Park every day after school, three hours on weekends, and four hours each day during summer vacation. The only time the youngsters were excused was when they were sick or it was raining.

Tennis

PRACTICING

There are probably more teaching aids available in tennis than in any other sport. If you have the budget, you can fill the back yard with equipment. A practice board, sometimes called a backboard or bounce-board, is one of the most practical items. It consists of a 12-foot-high wood panel as wide as a singles court. A white stripe running 3 feet above ground level indicates the net top. Several circular targets, each about 12 inches in diameter, are painted above the net line. Detailed instructions on how to build a practice board are available from the USLTA. You can buy "boards" of lightweight metal or tightly stretched netting, although these are substantially smaller than singles-court width.

Using the practice board, a young player will hit as many balls in ten minutes as he's likely to in an entire set of competitive play. It is especially good in helping a child develop his ground strokes, provided he's able to get sufficient distance from the board when he hits. The problem with backboard practice is that the ball always comes back the same way, or close to it, while one's opponent never hits two shots just alike. Confidence built from hitting off the board can be quickly shattered on the court.

The Swedes invented a device called the Tretorn Trainer which is meant to sharpen a player's footwork. It consists of a tennis ball attached to a long rubber cord, which in turn is attached to a heavy circular base, about the size of a big soup plate. Hit the ball and it snaps back for you to hit again. The cost: $13.

A much more elaborate training device is the Strokemaster, an electrically driven ball thrower which feeds a player a variety of shots, from sizzling serves and drives to tricky lobs and drop shots. It costs $395.

When your youngster practices with a partner, be certain that he is serious-minded about it. If he is too relaxed in his practice sessions, he may find it difficult to concentrate during a match. He should practice improving his weak points, not just exploit his strengths. Only in this way can he build his skill and confidence.

Of course, the only way a beginner can really learn the game is by means of on-the-court instruction, but novices can also benefit from the many fine tennis instruction books available. Among those frequently recommended are: *The Book of Tennis,* by Cornel Lumiere (Grosset & Dunlap, $1.95); *Beginning Tennis,* by Peter Everett and Virginia Skill (Wadsworth, $1.65); and *Use Your Head in Tennis,* by Bob Harman and K. Monroe (Kennikat, $2.50).

Girls enjoy and can profit from the very readable *Tennis to Win,* by Billie Jean King and Kim Chapin (Harper and Row, $5.95). *The Education of a Tennis Player,* by Rod Laver and Bud Collins (Simon and Schuster, $7.95), is a colorful autobiography.

THE USLTA

If your youngster becomes at all serious about tennis, be certain to investigate the benefits to be derived from a junior membership in the U.S. Lawn Tennis Association (51 East 42nd St., New York, N.Y. 10017). The annual fee is $4.

Membership makes the young player eligible for participation in sanctioned tournaments and qualifies him or her for possible ranking. The tournament program is all-embracing, involving both sexes, all ages (five different classifications up to eighteen), four different playing surfaces (grass, clay, hard court and indoor) and city, state, sectional and national competition. It comes to about 10,000 tournaments a year.

Membership also entitles the young player to a year's subscription to *Tennis, U.S.A.,* the USLTA's monthly magazine. It contains feature articles and helpful instruction tips.

The USLTA has available scores of books and booklets on the subjects of junior competition and tennis instructions. Films and slide programs are also available. Write to the USLTA's Education and Research Committee (71 University Place, Princeton, N.J. 08540) and request an official publication list and price sheet.

Much of the USLTA's tournament and instruction activity is of a sectional nature. You may want to contact your particular section for information.

The various sections of the USLTA are as follows:

Eastern Lawn Tennis Association
30 East 42nd St.
New York, N.Y. 10017

Intermountain Tennis Association
P.O. Box 2009
Salt Lake City, Utah 84110

Middle Atlantic Tennis Association
3035 Edgewood Ave.
Baltimore, Md. 21234

Tennis

Middle States Lawn Tennis Association
1311 Garden Lane
Reading, Penna. 19602

Missouri Valley Tennis Association
2237 Edgemont Ave.
Waterloo, Iowa 50702

Texas Tennis Association
3406 West Lamar St.
Houston, Tex. 77010

Southwestern Tennis Association
405 Lawyers Title Bldg.
Tucson, Ariz. 85701

Southern Lawn Tennis Association
3121 Maple Dr. N.E., Room 21-B
Atlanta, Ga. 30305

Pacific Northwest Lawn Tennis Association
2753 West 29th Ave.
Vancouver, B.C., Canada

Southern California Tennis Association
609 North Cahuenga Blvd.
Los Angeles, Calif. 90004

Northwestern Lawn Tennis Association
975 Northwestern Bank Building
Minneapolis, Minn. 55402

Hawaii Tennis Association
P.O. Box 411
Honolulu, Hawaii 96809

Florida Lawn Tennis Association
Box 790
Hallandale, Fla. 33009

Western Tennis Association
316 Charlotte Ave.
Royal Oak, Mich. 48075

New England Lawn Tennis Association
22 Wilde Rd.
Wellesley, Mass. 02181

Northern California Tennis Association
P.O. Box 337
Moraga, Calif. 94556

BADMINTON

Badminton is one sport that a child can play with success from the first day—that is, if you define "success" as the ability to have fun. The weight of the racket—about 5 ounces—is never a problem, and swinging it is a breeze. The bird, or shuttlecock, is not hard to hit over the net, and, since it decelerates so quickly in flight, it doesn't go out of bounds as readily as a tennis ball.

Yet, if you have played the game, you know that there are subtleties to badminton that a child will never begin to appreciate. The court, as compared to that for other racket games, is small, and consequently shots (in singles) must be struck with pinpoint accuracy.

Stamina is also important. The rules of the game state that the bird must be struck before it touches the ground or floor, which means, if one is up against a canny opponent, it must be pursued before each stroke. Add to this the fact that in a normal rally between skilled players the bird can cross the net twenty or twenty-five times, and you have clear evidence as to why endurance is so necessary.

Badminton can be played indoors or outdoors, but the outdoor version is less exacting. Because the bird is feather-light, it can be shunted off course by the gentlest of breezes.

Badminton

At every level, from novice to national champion, the game is challenging. Few sports are so valuable in keeping one in sound condition. And, of course, badminton has carry-over value; anyone from "six to sixty" can play.

One problem with badminton is a lack of facilities. Look in the Yellow Pages of your phone directory, and if there is a listing for "Badminton Courts" then you live in an unusual community. However, if you have sufficient space, you can set up an outdoor court. For singles play, the court measures 17 by 44 feet; for doubles it's 20 by 44 feet. Of course, for playing room you'll also need several additional feet at each end and on both sides.

EQUIPMENT

Get your child a racket that he can grip comfortably and swing easily. They are classified as light, medium, or heavy. A racket of average weight ranges from 4½ to 5 ounces.

He should be able to grip the handle firmly. Look for a handle that is eight-sided rather than round. This type will enable him to get a firmer grip, and the ridges will also serve to indicate to him, without looking, whether or not his grip is right.

Like tennis rackets, badminton rackets are now available in metal as well as wood. For a beginner, a steel-shafted racket, which will cost about $15, is best. It's both responsive and durable. Nylon stringing, while not considered to be quite as good as gut, is perfectly all right for the novice, and it lasts longer.

There are two types of birds—feather, with a cork base, and plastic, with a rubber base. The feathered type, because of the angled placement of the feathers, rotates as it flies, and thus is more likely to keep to a true course. It is best for precision play, and advanced players use no other kind.

The advantage of the plastic bird is that it can withstand quite a beating. Indeed, they last almost indefinitely, and that's why they are recommended for play between novices. Plastic birds cost from $2 to $4 for six, while quality feathered birds cost from $5 to $10 for six.

Advanced players pay close attention to what a bird weighs. The rules of the game set the weight at from 73 to 85 grains. The average weight is 76 grains. The late Ken Davidson, one of the sport's giants, said that a single grain added about 4 inches to the flight of a fully stroked bird. The shape of the feathers also has an effect on the distance the bird flies. A bird with pointed feathers flies farther than one with rounded feathers, provided they are of equal weight.

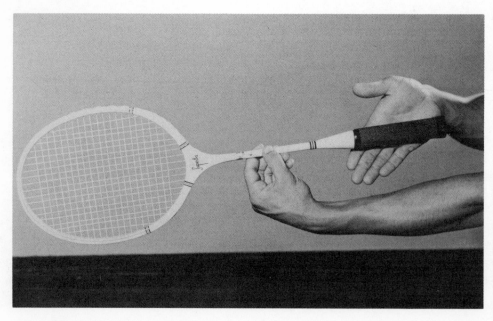

Badminton

Some firms market badminton sets, which are fine if your family is just taking up the sport. General Sportcraft Company, for example, sells a package that includes four tempered steel rackets, two plastic birds, a net and the net posts. The cost: about $20.

Clothing for badminton should be loose and comfortable. Buy tennis shoes, paying particular attention to the tread. For indoor play, a rubber sole is recommended; for play outdoors, a ridged sole.

DEVELOPING SKILLS

It takes plenty of practice to develop the deft stroking ability that good badminton requires. The skills involved aren't something the young player is likely to develop through competition, where the emphasis is on doing what's expedient.

Hitting a bird off a high wall (with a line on it at net height, 5 feet above the ground) is a good way to practice. This enables a player to drill on all the different strokes—forehands and backhands, overheads and underhands, drops, serves and smashes. Four or five practice sessions a week, each about half an hour in length, will help develop a young player's wrists. A quick, deft wrist snap is essential to badminton success.

Hitting off a wall also helps to improve one's reflexes. The player has to anticipate where the return "stroke" is going, and move to get it.

Of course, practicing with a partner is recommended, too. As is the case with any sport, any badminton practice session should be well planned. If you're practicing with your son, hit him a series of high serves, as many as fifteen or twenty of them, hitting alternately to his backhand and forehand. Let him return them with smashes (don't bother retrieving the birds).

Or you can hit him a series of low serves and have him rush to return each one. Or you can each take a midcourt position and exchange drives. Several minutes of practice should be devoted to each type of shot during each session.

Spend time working on his weaknesses, too. A smash aimed at his belt buckle is likely to be one. Many beginners have an inability to hit serves or clears deep enough. And often their serves trace too high an arc over the net.

Another problem that young players have, and one that practice isn't going to help much, has to do with patience, or lack of it. The capacity calmly to hit back shot after shot after shot, waiting for the opportunity to place the bird exactly where you want to, is as much of a factor in winning as dexterity and stamina. How do you teach a young player to be patient? By example. If you are impetuous, your son or daughter will be, too.

BADMINTON CLUBS

Joining a badminton club is the best way to enjoy the sport and improve your game and your youngster's. There are approximately 180 clubs and 4,000 players affiliated with the American Badminton Association (1330 Alexandria Dr., San Diego, Calif. 92107), the sport's governing body. Most clubs are located in or near major cities. Individual membership costs $5, but only $1.75 if you join through a club and $1 for juniors.

Each year the ABA sponsors badminton's Junior Nationals. Competition is in three age groups: thirteen and under, fifteen and under, and eighteen and under.

BOOKS AND PUBLICATIONS

The *Book of Badminton* (J. B. Lippincott, $4.95), by champion J. Frank Devlin, a volume from the Sports Illustrated Library, gives a clearcut explanation of the game's techniques. It offers chapters on grips, serves, clears, the smash, and singles and doubles tactics.

The official rules of badminton are available from the ABA (for 25¢), and the organization's bimonthly magazine, *Badminton USA* (which costs $3 a year) features information on tournaments and the rules, and gives instruction tips.

TABLE TENNIS

Table tennis—never "ping-pong" any more—is a different sport today than it was a couple of decades ago. It's different because of the racket.

Up until the mid-1950s, the racket was simply a saucer-shaped piece of plywood, covered on both sides with a layer of stippled rubber. Rackets of this type weighed between 4½ and 5¾ ounces.

The rackets that are popular today are the same size and about the same weight, but the wood is covered with a layer of sponge rubber, about two millimeters thick. Over this a second layer of rubber is fixed. This outer layer may have either a smooth rubbery finish or the familiar rubber pips.

In other words, there are three types of rackets you should know about. There is the "old" racket with its hard rubber pips, a type which is known as the "normal rubber" racket. The two modern types are known as the "inverted sponge" and the "sandwich sponge." The inverted-sponge is the smooth-surfaced racket. It gets the name "inverted" because the rubber pips face downward. Unless you look closely, you don't even know they're there. In the sandwich-sponge racket, the pips face upward. (There are also rackets faced on each surface with cork or sandpaper, but these types are not recognized by the game's governing body, the U.S. Table Tennis Association.)

With the old racket, table tennis was largely a defensive game, and patience was the chief quality a championship player required. It was plick-pluck, plick-pluck, plick-pluck until someone made a mistake. Not any more. The new rackets have made it an attacking game. When the ball strikes a sponge racket, the effect is the same as when a person jumps onto a trampoline feet first. The ball sinks into the layer of rubber and the cushion of sponge underneath, then explodes away with a tricky spin.

The disadvantage of the sponge rackets has to do with control. You can't pinpoint your shots as you can with a normal rubber racket, but this drawback is more than outweighed by the advantages of sponge.

Which type of racket should a youngster use? The inverted-sponge racket, the type with a smooth rubbery surface, the pips facing downward. "If I were coaching a twelve-year-old boy, a good athlete, in hope of turning out a world champion," says former champion Dick Miles in his book *The Game of Table Tennis,* "I would start him off using the inverted sponge . . . not have him build up to it."

Sponge rackets cost $8 to $15 and can be purchased almost anywhere sporting goods are sold. A racket cover to protect the bat costs about $2.

Unlike rackets of days gone by, the sponge racket does not last indefinitely. The sponge loses its resiliency and a new racket has to be purchased or the sponge replaced. You can buy small square "sandwiches" of rubber and paddle sponge to enliven an old racket. Simply take the old rubber off, trim the new to fit the paddle, and stick it in place (it's self-sticking). Replacement rubber costs about $4 a square. One company recommends that paddle sponge be replaced after sixty hours of play.

Once you've decided upon a racket type, let your youngster grip and swing rackets of different weights and handle shapes until he finds one that feels comfortable. Beware of what the USTTA calls "junky" equipment, the type usually sold in kit form, the kit containing two or four rackets, balls, and a net. The highest-quality table tennis equipment that you can buy costs only a few dollars more than the cheapest.

When you buy table tennis balls, look for the USTTA or ITTF (International Table Tennis Federation) seal of approval. Then you know that you're getting balls of tournament quality.

BUYING A TABLE

Table tennis is unique because you can purchase a table, set it up in a room that is big enough and light it properly, and then enjoy the very same conditions that prevail at major tournaments right in your own home. Few other sports are so suited. Try it with bowling and it will cost you $15,000, and you'd better have a very long room.

The table—5 by 9 feet—should be at least ¾ inch thick. Again, look for USTTA or ITTF endorsement. A pressed-wood table is regarded as being superior to the plywood kind because the latter may contain some "dead" spots where the ball doesn't bounce right. If you do buy plywood, however, be sure you get at least five-ply plywood.

Some types of tables fold for storage. Others have wheels so you can move them about. The surface of the table, no matter the type, should be 2½ feet from the floor.

You can also purchase a table with a "playback" feature. One half of the playing surface can be tilted up at right angles to the other half, which enables a player to practice by himself. Tables range in price from $50 to $150.

Examine the net. USTTA regulations specify that it should be 6 feet in length, and thus project 6 inches beyond each side of the table. The net is suspended from the net posts by a cord that runs through the top binding. Net tension can be regulated by adjusting the cord at either end.

You need plenty of space around the table. The USTTA recommends an open area of 6 feet on each side of the table, and 12 feet at each end. The ceiling should be 12 feet in height, although you can make do with less.

Be sure that you have adequate lighting. For tournament play, light intensity of 30 footcandles at the table surface is required. This translates into four light fixtures, each with a 300-watt bulb and 14-inch reflector, mounted at a height of at least 12 feet above the table surface. Again, less can be adequate.

SOME BASICS

Most instructors will tell you that it's better to teach a young player to use the conventional handshake grip, rather than what is known as the penholder grip. With the handshake grip, the base of the racket blade is grasped between the thumb and forefinger of the right hand; the fingers close about the handle. The thumb side is toward the player anytime he executes a backhand stroke. The other side is used for forehand strokes.

In the case of the penholder grip, the handle of the racket is held in somewhat the same manner one grips a pen or pencil. The forefinger and thumb encircle the racket handle and extend over the base of the blade, while the three fingers give support from the other side.

Table Tennis

Although the penholder grip is used by many champion players, it's not a good grip to teach novices. It's difficult—indeed, impossible—to execute background strokes when using the penholder grip, and this, naturally, limits one's ability to attack and defend. Players who have been successful with the style boast incredible agility, darting into position so quickly that they are able to get what would ordinarily be a backhand stroke from the other side of the table, the forehand side. In other words, all their strokes are forehand strokes.

Table tennis is different from other racket sports in that ball spin is of critical importance. (Of course, it's important in lawn tennis, too, but not as far as novices are concerned. The basic reason is that the ball is so light in weight—it weighs only 2½ grams—that the effects

of even the smallest amount of spin are readily apparent, either in the manner in which the ball curves in flight or the eccentric arc it takes off a bounce.

There are several different kinds of spin. A player can impart forward, backward or side spin, depending on how he grazes his racket over the surface of the ball.

Young players often have two misconceptions about the game, both of them involving the serve. The first has to do with where the serve is to be placed. Often there's a tendency to confuse table tennis with lawn tennis and the server tries to place the ball in the court diagonally opposite. Players do this because they're puzzled by the white stripe that runs down the center of the table, dividing it in half, so that with the net there seem to be four courts. But the white stripe has no meaning in singles play; it relates to doubles only. In singles play, the serve, after striking on the server's side of the table, can be hit to *any part* of the opponent's side.

Few novice players know the rulebook method of serving. First of all, the serve has to be executed from a point behind the table end. It's also mandatory that the ball be held in the palm of the hand; in fact, the rulebook says in the *center* of the palm. With the hand flat, the player tosses the ball straight upward, then swings through. He can serve from either the backhand or forehand side. When a served ball touches the net in passing over, it must be played over.

A player serves for five consecutive points, then receives for five consecutive points, and the game continues in that fashion until one player reaches 21 points. Should the score become 20-20, the service changes after every ensuing point until one player gains a two-point advantage, i.e., 23-21, 24-22, etc.

COMPETITION AND THE USTTA

Those whose experience in table tennis is limited to competition in their own homes or the homes of friends are often referred to as "basement players." Once your youngster is ready to graduate from this category, find out whether there is a USTTA-affiliated club or league in operation in your area. These are listed in the USTTA's official publication, *Table Tennis Topics,* or you can consult your Yellow Pages under the listing "Table Tennis Courts," then call and inquire. There are about 150 table tennis clubs affiliated with the USTTA. If there happens to be one in your community, you are likely to find that it offers both junior league and junior tournament competition.

Table Tennis

Besides sanctioning league and tournament play, the USTTA administers the game's rules and regulations, sponsors U.S. players in international events, conducts regional tournaments and an annual national tournament, and distributes instructional booklets and films. A one-year junior membership in the USTTA, which makes the holder eligible for tournament competition, costs $2. Members receive a free subscription to *Table Tennis Topics,* the organization bimonthly newspaper. The USTTA's address is Box 815, Orange, Conn. 06477.

BOOKS AND PUBLICATIONS

When the United States table tennis team was invited to visit the People's Republic of China in April 1971, it led to an easing of tensions between East and West, what the press referred to as an era of "ping-pong diplomacy." It also triggered a boom in table tennis and, about a year after, a boom in table tennis instruction books. The best book, however, is not one of these, but a volume that was published several years before.

Titled *The Game of Table Tennis* (J. B. Lippincott, $6.50), it is the work of Dick Miles, a ten-time U.S. Champion but, more important, a skilled player with the ability to analyze the game with precision and clarity. He examines the grip, the subject of spin, and then the form and technique of each of the principal strokes. Excellent drawings illustrate the text.

For a rundown of the game's rules, write the USTTA and ask for a copy of the booklet titled "Table Tennis for You." It also contains basic instructional information.

OTHER COURT GAMES

Racquets, squash and squash tennis are members of the tennis family. The idea in each is to keep the ball in play until your opponent misses. Each game is played with a racket. Handball, though not played with a racket, is also basically a modification of tennis.

Each of these games puts a stress on quick reflexes and agility. A beginner can often have as much fun as a seasoned expert. The only drawback is that the facilities for playing these games are few, being limited to athletic clubs, country clubs and some colleges.

RACQUETS

Facilities for racquets are available in private clubs in New York, Philadelphia and Boston. Elsewhere the game is little known.

The racquet itself has a long, slim handle and circular head, about 8 inches in diameter. The ball is made of tightly wound twine covered with leather, is 1 inch in diameter, and weighs about an ounce.

The racquet court consists of an enclosed rectangular space 60 by 30 feet, with front and side walls 30 feet high and back wall 15 feet high. Markings on the floor and front wall indicate where a serve must be directed.

Other Court Games

The first player to score 15 points wins the game. The server can score a point, called an "ace," as in other court games. To win an exchange, a player must be the last to hit the ball legally, so that the ball hits the front wall before striking the floor. In match play three out of five games is usually the basis for victory.

SQUASH

The game of squash, also commonly known as squash racquets, was derived from racquets. But whereas racquets is always played indoors, squash, because the court is smaller and less elaborate, can be played outdoors as well as in.

Squash mushroomed in popularity in the 1920s. It still has pockets of adherents on the Pacific Coast, the Middle West and, of course, the Northeast. Eastern colleges—Harvard, Yale and Princeton in particular—have always been squash strongholds.

The squash racket looks like a very sturdy badminton racket. It cannot be longer than 27 inches. The circular head is about 7 inches in diameter. The racket weighs between 8 and 10 ounces. The ball is hollow black rubber and about the size of a golf ball, 1¾ inches in diameter. It weighs about 1 ounce.

The squash court is 32 feet long and 18½ feet wide. Three walls are 15 feet high, while the back wall is 7 feet high.

On the front wall, there is a service line 6½ feet from the floor. Running along the bottom of the front wall is a metal telltale, which is 17 inches high. The telltale's metallic ring tells the players a shot is not good. Floor markings indicate service boxes.

Whoever wins an exchange gets the point. The winner of the point serves the next point. One service fault is enough to lose the point. To win, a player must score 15 points.

The rules for doubles are much the same. The first partner on one side serves until he loses a point, then the other partner serves until he loses a point.

The rules and court specifications for squash have been standardized through the efforts of the U.S. Squash Racquets Association (4318 Far Hill Dr., Bloomfield Hills, Mich. 48013). The organization also conducts squash tournaments and promotes a variety of junior activities. Women's competition is supervised by the U.S. Women's Squash Racquets Association (42 Dudley Lane, Milton, Mass. 02186).

29

SQUASH TENNIS

Squash tennis is played on a squash court. The ball is bigger and much livelier and can carom around the court in bewildering fashion. Quick reactions are a must. The racket is sturdier than the racket used in squash, resembling a sawed-off tennis racket.

The National Squash Tennis Association (Box 14, 15 West 43rd St., New York, N.Y. 10036) has codified the rules of the sport. The organization also sponsors exhibitions, instruction clinics and tournaments.

HANDBALL

Physical fitness experts give handball the highest marks. The sport ranks with basketball and squash as an oxygen-producing exercise.

Handball can be played indoors or outdoors by two or four players. The handball itself is made of black rubber. It is 1⅞ inches in diameter and weighs about 2 ounces.

In one-wall handball, the wall is 16 feet high, and the court 20 feet wide and 34 feet long. Rules for the four-wall game call for three 20-foot walls and a 10-foot back wall. The four-wall court is 20 feet wide and 40 feet long.

To begin a game, the server drops the ball on the floor, and on the rebound strikes it with his hand. The serve must strike the front wall first and on the rebound must hit the floor behind what is known as the short line. The opposing player may play the ball on the fly or first bounce. Opponents strike alternately until one fails to make a good return. Only the server can score; his opponent can win only the right to serve. The game is won by the first player scoring 21 points.

Handball became popular in the United States after World War I, thanks to the promotion efforts of the AAU and YMCA. Both of these organizations sponsor national championships today, as does the U.S. Handball Association (4101 Dempster St., Skokie, Ill. 60076). This organization supports junior tournament activity and publishes an annual directory and a bimonthly magazine, *Handball.*

II INDIVIDUAL SPORTS

GOLF
SKIING
RIDING
ICE SKATING
FENCING
BOWLING
ARCHERY

GOLF

Is golf a good sport for a youngster to play? There's debate about it.

Dr. Hans Kraus, an associate professor of rehabilitation medicine at the New York University Medical Center, and a member of the President's Council on Physical Fitness, criticizes golf as being emotionally detrimental to young players. "A youngster needs strenuous physical exercise in order to release tension," he says. "But from what I've seen golf relieves nervous tension for very few players. Most people get more tense as they are playing."

There are those who dispute Dr. Kraus' findings. Arnold Palmer, for instance, agrees that golf can build up tension in a child, but he doesn't feel that it is necessarily detrimental. "Golf," says Palmer, "teaches the child how to deal with tensions, how to handle himself when he becomes tense in certain situations." In other words, Palmer feels that by constantly exposing the young player to tension-producing situations, golf helps to build emotional maturity.

Perhaps, then, it all comes down to the child himself, to his temperament. There are children who can grip the club firmly and hit the ball straight and far, but lack the emotional development that golf competition demands. There are others who can cope with the emotional rigors of the game—indeed, youngsters whose emotional development will benefit from it.

Dr. Kraus also rejects golf as an activity that will produce physical fitness. Youngsters, he says, need *vigorous* activity, and golf isn't vigorous enough. "If they have time for golf as well as bicycling, running, tennis, and other active things like that, then fine, I'd say keep on golfing," Dr. Kraus declared in an interview which appeared in *Golf* magazine. But if it takes away from their time for the activities they must have in order to build and maintain good physical fitness, then it's bad. And I think this is generally the case."

But this, too, depends to some extent on how the young golfer approaches the game. When Arnold Palmer was a child, he used to hit a small bucket of balls, run out and pick them up, run back to the tee, and hit them again. He did this for two or three hours a day. He also played a round or two each day. For Palmer the sport was something more than a mild workout.

When it comes to the physical attributes a golfer needs, it helps to be slender and tall. Tallness implies long legs and long arms, and hence a greater swing arc, more power. But boys who are small can do well if they happen to be very well coordinated. Chi Chi Rodriguez, one of the game's longest hitters in the early 1970s, weighed only about 128 pounds. Gary Player is probably an even better example. Once, by his own admission, "a 98-pound weakling," Gary built himself up by a diligent weightlifting program and exercises like finger-tip pushups. Be wary here, however. Golf requires long and supple muscles, not bulging ones. If your youngster plans to lift weights to improve his swing power, be sure he's under the supervision of a knowledgeable instructor.

EQUIPMENT AND FUNDAMENTALS

All of the major golf equipment companies make special sets of clubs for young players. The idea is for the child to use the junior set until he becomes bigger and more proficient. Junior clubs are lighter and have shorter shafts than adult models. A junior set is not a complete set. It usually includes the 1 and 3 woods, the 3, 5, 7 and 9 irons, and a putter. Such sets, with the bag included, cost from $50 to $75.

Of all the club makers, Spalding has taken the most reasoned approach toward young players. The firm offers two sets of clubs for juniors, one for the child who is 4-feet-8 or under (consisting of a driver, the 5, 7 and 9 irons, and a putter), and a second set that has slightly longer shafts and is slightly heavier for the youngster whose height ranges from 4-feet-8 to 5-feet-4 (consisting of the 1 and 3 woods, the

Golf

3, 5, 7, and 9 irons, and a putter). Both sets have tempered steel shafts; the irons have chrome-plated faces, and the woods, for durability, have fiberglass heads.

If you have a set of your own clubs that you have discarded, ask at your local pro shop about having the shafts cut down to suit your child. Many parents do this. Remember, the child doesn't require a full set; generally, just the odd-numbered clubs.

One of the benefits to be derived from using an abridged set is that the youngster will be forced to learn to hit quarter-, half- and three-quarter shots. Later on, when he begins using a full set, this is still a good skill to have.

Don't allow a youngster to grab a club and start hitting balls off the practice tee using the same grip he uses on his baseball bat or hockey stick. Get him to grip the club properly right from the start. Take him to the club pro or any teaching professional.

The type of grip he's taught will depend on the strength of his hands and the length of his fingers. A very young boy whose hands are small and haven't acquired their full strength should use a ten-finger grip (not to be confused with the so-called baseball grip). There's no overlapping or interlocking in the usual sense. The fingers encircle the club with the little finger of the right hand snuggled up against the curled forefinger of the left hand.

The thumbs are on the shaft, not wrapped around it. This means that the last three fingers of the right hand, as they curl around the shaft, will come in contact with the left thumb or may even encircle it. The hands tend to work as a single unit, and this is what makes the ten-finger grip superior to the normal baseball grip in which each hand grips independently of the other.

Many youngsters can be taught the interlocking grip right from the start, even those with small hands. In this, the little finger of the right hand is interlocked between the forefinger and second finger of the left hand. Here both hands do function as a unit.

The child whose fingers are too small for the standard overlapping grip can be taught the Vardon grip. In the Vardon grip, the little finger of the right hand overlaps the forefinger of the left hand. While there is no doubt that the overlapping style produces the surest, firmest grip, and thus gives the greatest potential for a powerful swing, it is sometimes troublesome for the young player. The little finger of the right hand (the finger that does the overlapping) may have an unnatural "feel" to it, causing a buildup of tension in the right wrist. If this happens, all kind of things can go awry. But with the ten-finger grip, which

feels much more natural to most young players, the problem of tension isn't likely to develop. What it boils down to is that the overlapping grip may take some getting used to.

Once you've decided upon a grip and your youngster is swinging the club, encourage him to practice with the short irons, the 9 iron and 7 iron. Most youngsters want to boom out drives right from the start or spend their practice time putting, but both of these can wait. What you want at the outset is for him to get the "feel" of a club, and the way to do this is by having him hit short finesse shots. The driver is the very last club that he should attempt to use.

Many instructors, once the young player's grip is settled upon, concentrate on balance. If a youngster is properly balanced as he swings, he is much more likely to be properly coordinated. Forget about whether his stance is supposed to be open or closed; just encourage him to stand naturally, his feet square to the ball. Have him hit all his shots off his left foot. Drill him in this fashion for a couple of weeks. He'll not only learn balance but should begin developing a hip swing and pivot as well.

Girls have little difficulty learning how to grip the club, and the stance is seldom a problem and neither is balance, but the swing itself is another matter. Some girls bring the club back awkwardly, and the result is a swing that has a freakish look to it.

Often the problem is that the girl hasn't found her own swing plane. Some people should be almost upright as they swing, others require an almost flat swing, and still others should swing on a plane that's in between these two.

A good way to check a girl's swing is to place a golf club opposite her and just beyond the ball as she addresses it, placing the club handle so that it lies parallel to the intended flight of the ball. Then check her swing from behind. At a point halfway through the backswing and again at the top of the backswing, her club should be parallel to the club on the ground. After hitting, her arms should be extended toward her target and again her club should be parallel to the club on the ground. If she is not getting the two clubs parallel at each of these three checkpoints, she's taking the club back too far to either the inside or outside. The plane of her swing has to be adjusted.

If a youngster has an aptitude for the game, it will show early. Jack Nicklaus was ten years old when his father arranged for him to receive lessons from professional Jack Grout of the Scioto Country Club near Columbus, Ohio. The first time on the course, Jack shot a 61 for the first nine holes, a 50 for the second nine. The next summer, at eleven, he was winning trophies and beating sixteen-year-olds to do it. At thirteen, Nicklaus twice shot three-under-par 69s at Scioto, a fine course, and three years later he won the Ohio Open, the youngest player ever to do so.

IMPROVING SKILLS

There are many things that you can do to help improve your child's golf game. You can provide him with a junior membership at the club. You can arrange a series of lessons for him from the pro. You can send him to a golf clinic or a camp.

Another thing you can do, and it costs nothing—indeed, he'll be paid for it—is let him caddy. Most pros on the tour today caddied as youngsters, and virtually all of them feel the experience was beneficial. The caddy, simply by observing, learns a great deal about the rules and golf etiquette, and when he happens to be caddying for experienced players, much about how to play the game. Another advantage is that clubs permit their caddies to play the course on Monday morning or some other "off" time during the week.

Golf

Lew Worsham, in an article in *Golf* magazine, pointed out that at one time, before college golf became the principal training ground, all of the leading pros were former caddies. The reason, said Worsham, was because every caddy, while waiting for an assignment, would chip constantly—in the grass, over roots, out of the sand. "The result was," Worsham declared, "that he developed a 'feel' of doing things with the golf ball and making it react." One good thing about the short pitch-and-run with the 7 iron and maybe even a pitch with the 9 iron is that there may be room enough in your backyard for practicing.

A driving range can be useful as a place to practice—if it's used thoughtfully. Many players use the range simply to belt the ball, trying to establish how far they can hit it. But range practice should have a purpose to it. Be sure your youngster uses his own clubs, golf shoes, and, if he wears one, a golf glove.

Practicing shot control is a good way to use the range. Have the youngster hit high and low hooks and high and low fades, and have him hit low and straight. If he can learn to place a ball exactly where he wants it, he'll be getting something worthwhile out of these practice sessions.

When Lee Trevino was learning the game, he and his friends would play several types of range games to prevent the sessions from becoming boring. "We'd shoot at yardage markers for a quarter," he once recalled. "The closest to the sign would win two bits. Or we'd try to hit the ball in between the two posts supporting a yard marker. This was worth a dollar." Besides earning pocket money, Trevino was learning how to hit low and straight.

There are from fifteen to twenty golf camps in operation, offering summertime instruction for boys (there are no girls' camps yet) aged twelve to sixteen at fees that range to about $1,250 for an eight-week course. Each camp is staffed by a corps of instructors headed by a qualified pro. Usually there is one instructor for every nine or ten youngsters.

It's usual for the morning hours to be given over to instruction, although the amount of individual attention a boy receives varies with his skill and experience. Afternoons are devoted to playing. Tournaments are held frequently during sessions to give the youngsters competitive experience. Camps also emphasize sportsmanship and golf etiquette.

INSTRUCTION AIDS

Golf instruction books have been written by just about every professional who has ever won a tournament, and by a good number of those who haven't. The result is selection that can't help but bewilder you. One book, however, continues to remain pre-eminent. It's Ben Hogan's *Five Lessons: The Modern Fundamentals of Golf* (A. S. Barnes, $4.95). Written in collaboration with Herbert Warren Wind and illustrator Anthony Ravielli, the book is unusual because of the clarity with which it explains both the theory and technique of the grip and swing. Studying it can't help but make you a better teacher and your son or daughter a better golfer.

A splendid supplementary text is the 44-page book titled *Golf Lessons,* which is available for $1 from the National Golf Foundation (Merchandise Mart, Chicago, Ill. 60654). A set of twelve fully developed golf lessons—The Grip, The Swing, Putting, Playing a Hole, etc.—it's a book that has been used successfully to introduce beginners to the game and by professional instructors as a teaching reference. It is easy to read and understand, and it features more than 100 illustrations by golf artist Dom Lupo.

The book presents exercises that a young player can perform at

Golf

home to help him improve the critical movements of his swing, and it also contains several pages of charts a youngster can use to record his progress.

The National Golf Foundation has available many other instructional aids, including a handbook titled *The Golf Instructor's Guide,* which contains advice on instruction techniques, exercises, practice facilities, etc. If you are playing an active role in the instruction of your youngster, it's sure to be helpful. The cost: $3.50.

In addition, the National Golf Foundation makes available golf instruction motion pictures, which can be purchased or rented, and several loop films, priced at $20 each. Each covers a different phase of golf instruction. Write the National Golf Foundation for additional information on films and instruction publications. They'll send you a free catalog.

For a copy of the rules of golf, write to the U.S. Golf Association (Far Hills, N.J. 07931). *Golf Rules in Pictures* (Grosset & Dunlap, $1.95) is easier for youngsters to understand.

SKIING

You can't teach a young boy or girl to play a round of golf with only a few hours of instruction, nor to swim or play tennis. But skiing is different—thanks to modern instruction methods.

I'm referring, of course, to the Graduated Length Method of teaching, or GLM as everyone calls it. The method starts the beginner on easy-to-handle short skis to give him the "feel" of skiing, and steps him up to midlength and then standard-length skis, all in only five or six lessons. It hasn't exactly revolutionized the sport, but it has shifted things around a little. It has made learning awfully easy, and fun.

Children like skiing because it is a spirited, action-filled sport. It gives a sense of derring-do. Once a youngster knows what it feels like to whiz down the side of a mountain, he'll never spend another snowy afternoon watching television.

BUYING EQUIPMENT

Take your time picking out equipment for your child. Not only does his enjoyment of the sport depend on the buying decisions you make, but his safety does, too. Make a mistake in purchasing him a set of golf clubs, and he may end up only hooking his drives. But with ski equipment it could mean a winter spent in a hospital bed.

Skiing

One problem with purchasing ski equipment is that it changes so frequently, and what is available in the way of skis, boots and bindings today no more resembles what was available a decade or so ago than the current Fords and Chevrolets resemble the Jeep. If you skied as a youngster, you probably used wood skis. Everyone once did. But today's skis are frequently made of fiberglass or metal. And remember how you used to struggle lacing boots. Well, boots don't lace any more; they buckle.

If your child has some reservations about skiing, or if you just want to see how he takes to the sport, provide him with rental equipment at first. Most ski areas and the larger equipment shops rent boots, skis, bindings and poles on a per-day or per-weekend basis. You can completely outfit a child for about $10 to $15 a day.

But rental equipment is less than ideal. The skis may not be exactly the right length nor have the degree of flexibility the child requires, and the boots may not give his ankles the support he needs. If you feel your child is serious about skiing and is going to be on the slopes frequently, it's much better to buy him his own gear.

If you're not an experienced skier with a complete knowledge of equipment, make your purchases in a ski shop or sporting-goods store, a place where the sales personnel will include a skier or two. Look for shops in the Yellow Pages under ''Ski Equipment—Retail.'' Avoid discount stores, where the clerks think a stem is part of a flower. Of course, if you know brand names and prices, you can shop anywhere. One good way to become informed is to consult the yearbooks and buying guides published each fall by *Ski Magazine* and *Skiing Magazine.* You can order back issues by mail.

Purchase the youngster's boots first, then the skis, bindings, poles, and whatever accessory equipment he might require. One way to keep costs down is to deal with a ski shop that offers a trade-in policy. When the child outgrows his boots, they serve as part payment on a larger size. Some ski shops offer this arrangement on skis and poles, too. But be sure your youngster takes care of his equipment. Otherwise, the trade-in value will be nil.

You can also keep down the cost of equipment if you can find out about a ''ski swap.'' These are common to most snow communities. Usually held in the fall, a ski swap enables you to exchange with others the gear that your child has outgrown. Ask other parents if they know of any.

Boots. Boots are the most important piece of equipment your youngster will own, even more important than his skis. Boots should be of double-boot construction—that is, a rugged, ankle-supporting

outer boot enclosing an inner boot that hugs the foot. When the child goes for a fitting, be sure he brings along a pair of lightweight socks and a pair of heavy ones, the same as he'll be wearing on the slopes.

The boots must fit snugly but comfortably. Your youngster's toes may touch the inside of the boot toe when he first tries it on, but once it is buckled his foot should be forced back toward the boot heel, which will relieve the pressure up front. He should be able to wiggle his toes some, but the heel should remain firmly anchored. Hold the boot to the floor and have him try to raise the heel inside. There should be virtually no movement.

In general, what you are looking for are boots that are going to permit him to flex his ankles forward and back but at the same time give him plenty of lateral ankle support. Boots are not going to feel like shoes. Yet they should be comfortable and not exert undue pressure at any point. Be sure the boots have a rigid sole that resists twisting, have sturdy buckles, and are sufficiently padded.

Some parents buy boots that are slightly larger than actually needed with the idea that the child will grow into them. During the period of growth, the child wears an extra pair of socks. This plan is open to question. The matter of boot fit is critical to your child's development as a skier, and thus his enjoyment of the sport. It is not wise to make any compromises when it come to boots. And the saving isn't *that* much.

The very newest development is "foam-injected" boots. The buyer dons the boots and stands erect, and then a salesman pumps liquefied plastic foam into the boots through a valve at the back of the heel. The foam stiffens around the foot for a perfect fit. Other types used injected liquid wax instead of foam. Boots of this type are not cheap; they cost from $70 to $190. Consider them for your youngster only if he is *very* serious about the sport.

For a small child, try a plastic-laminated four-buckle boot with a nylon lining and a stiff PVC sole. The cost: $25 to $30. For the older youngster, there's Henke's "Junior Standard," which looks like an adult boot and, at $40, is priced like one.

The Nordica Alpina, made in Italy, is a good compromise between the standard boot and the foam type. Called a pre-foam boot, it is lined with foam rubber and gives a very snug fit but is feathery soft. The price is $50. Given proper care, a boot of this type has a high trade-in value.

Skis. If you are buying for a young beginner, skis are no great expense. For example, laminated wood skis, the top and sides painted plastic, the bottom a more durable sheet plastic, should not cost you more than $20 or $30, the precise cost depending on the length. They can be chin or nose high—that is, shorter than normal—which will give better control. When the child outgrows the skis or damages them beyond repair, buying a new pair won't put a great strain on the family budget.

If you're buying for an older child, a skilled skier, look for well-known brands that offer generous guarantee terms. This is true whether you are shopping for metal or fiberglass. The terms should include a reconditioning treatment for the top and bottom surfaces.

Skis for children should have a good amount of flexibility and camber. The latter term refers to the bow or arch of the skis. Put the skis together bottom-to-bottom. They will touch at the tips and tails but bend outward like an archer's bow. At the middle they should be from 1½ to 2 inches apart.

Head offers a junior ski known as the GK, which is becoming quite popular. Made of a foam core and single top layer of fiberglass, it is both light and flexible. It costs about $70.

Many instructors recommend metal skis for juniors, especially if the boy or girl skis a great deal. Being metal, they're much more durable; indeed, they're virtually unbreakable, and require little in the way of maintenance. But they cost more, up to $100.

What is the proper length ski for the young skier? There's no precise answer, no rule of thumb that you can follow. It depends on several factors, with the level of ability he's attained the most important one. If he can ski parallel and occasionally handle an "expert" slope, he needs a relatively long ski, much longer than if he happens to be just out of ski school and finds "intermediate" slopes a problem. It depends, too, on the youngster's height and weight. A boy or girl who is tall and of good size needs a longer-than-average ski.

A youngster of average ability, and of average height and weight, will probably do best with skis that are about six inches taller than he is. Only an expert ever uses skis that are as long as 200 cm. (6 feet 7 inches).

Bindings. Ski bindings have to hold the boots and the skier securely to his skis, but only up to a point. In the case of a fall, they must be sensitive enough to release the skis. Obviously you have to be careful when purchasing bindings.

Name-brand bindings cost $25 to $35, plus another $5 or so to have them mounted on the skis. Get quality bindings; don't compromise. Keep in mind that the youngster isn't going to wear out or outgrow them. Bindings can be used from one season to the next. You simply have them remounted when the youngster changes skis.

Many new bindings feature a heel unit that can be mounted to accommodate three or more boot sizes without the necessity of doing any remounting. The advantage is obvious.

The Spademan binding, designed by a California orthopedist, is one of the most promising developments in the field of ski safety in years. Instead of being attached in the conventional manner, at the heel and toe, the Spademan binding fastens beneath the arch. It releases even in slow, twisting falls, the type that sometimes fails to spring open the usual type of binding. At ski areas where they have been used, Spademan bindings have made a significant reduction in the injury rate.

No matter what type of bindings your child uses, they won't give him sufficient protection unless they're properly adjusted. Getting the right adjustment is a trial-and-error business. The first time he uses them have a ski-shop expert adjust them to the lightest possible setting for his weight and skiing proficiency. Then have him try the bindings at that setting. If they release too readily, have them tightened a bit, and then have him give them another try. Keep at it until you reach the point of equilibrium.

Poles. It's not wise to make a definite statement as to how long poles should be. The reason is that "expert" opinion on the topic keeps shifting. Just be sure that the poles your young skier picks out are long enough to help him climb a slope or turn on level terrain, but not so long that they get in his way on a downhill run. This probably means they'll be about armpit-high.

Durability is very important. Poles take a beating from young users.

Allow your child to handle and swing the poles to be certain they're well balanced and not too heavy. The straps should be good and wide so they won't cut into the wrists, and the strap loop should be big enough so that the pole can be grasped fully, even when heavy mittens are being worn.

Poles range in price from $5 to $20. With the higher-priced poles, the handle height is adjustable, a good feature if your youngster is growing fast.

Ski clothing. The "secret" to dressing for skiing is layered clothing. If your child wears windproof outer clothing over a few layers of woolen clothing, he can ski on the coldest day. He can also adjust the number of inner layers to suit whatever the thermometer happens to read.

If it is a cold day, the innermost layer should be thermal underwear. Over that goes pants, a shirt, and a couple of sweaters. Over these go a warm-up suit, an outer layer consisting of a parka and insulated pants with zippers running down the sides of the legs. A knitted wool hat and warm leather mittens complete the outfit. Dressed in this fashion, your son or daughter can ski in Siberia.

If your young skier is in his teens or approaching them, you won't have to give him any advice on ski fashions. He or she will know what's "in." Down-filled, fur-hooded Air Force jackets are one example of what's been popular in recent years. In areas where it's cold but not bitter, faded Levis are the thing. Jeans, however, aren't practical unless they've been waterproofed; use Scotchgard.

For the best selection of ski clothing, shop early, in August. For bargain prices, shop late, in March or April.

If your child wears prescription lenses, have him buy an elastic band that attaches to the ends of the bows and fits around the back of the head to prevent the glasses from being jarred loose. Such bands cost only a dollar or so at any sporting-goods store. Incidentally, be sure his lenses are unbreakable plastic, not glass. If he wants to wear sunglasses, there's no need to have them ground to his prescription. Simply get him a plastic visor to wear over his glasses. They come in many different shades.

SKIING INSTRUCTION

Short skis are easier to maneuver than long ones. This simple physical principle has led to some revolutionary developments in skiing instruction in recent years, specifically to the Graduated Length Method mentioned earlier. There's no better way to teach your child to ski.

While occasionally it happens that a ten-year-old can ski parallel after only five or six hours of instruction, GLM involves a five-day course. These can be five consecutive days, five consecutive Saturdays, or Saturdays and Sundays for three weekends. What appeals to youngsters about GLM is that it is action-oriented. There is no need for lectures or stationary drills at the bottom of the hill. Within a few hours, students are riding lifts and skiing downhill. By the end of their instructional week, they have the ability to ski parallel on skis of normal

Skiing

length and can negotiate several slopes at any average ski resort.

You don't have to buy equipment until the youngster is proficient. Everything is rented. The cost? About $50 for five lessons, and that includes the equipment rental.

GLM is not new. It's just taken a long time for the idea to catch on. Short "learning skis" were being used in Germany in the 1950s. For years they were promoted in this country by Clif Taylor, who began experimenting with the short ski at Hogback, Vermont, as early as 1959. He sold the first skis of graduated lengths, 3-, 4-, and 5-footers, under the name "Shortee Skis." "You can ski in a day," Taylor would tell potential customers. "You just twist your feet and then your skis. That's all there is to it."

The several GLM systems in use today are all similar in that they feature Taylor's basic principle—the direct turn. This is in contrast to the traditional snowplow and stem turns that beginners have been taught for generations.

Ski schools in every part of the country now feature one form or another of GLM. Most of those that don't have found it too expensive to stock skis in all those different sizes.

The alternative way is to learn on a single pair of 5-foot skis and use them to advance from beginner to near expert. It's just not as easy—nor as safe.

If you live in or close to a large city, inquire at ski shops about instruction programs for beginner skiers. Most offer special programs for young skiers, busing groups of them to a nearby ski area on weekend mornings or during vacation periods for instruction. Be sure your child is going to be with others of his age and ability.

In some areas of the country, youngsters learn to ski through the public school system. Individual classes are bused to the slope one afternoon a week during the snow season. Programs of this type are most common to the Pacific Coast and Rocky Mountain areas, although there is a sprinkling of them through New England.

Ski writer Mort Lund explains the short-ski teaching method in depth in his book *Ski GLM* (Dial Press, $7.95). He appraises each of the several GLM teaching systems and compares GLM with the more traditional approach. There's also a lengthy but lucid discussion on how to select skis of proper length. The book contains some 400 photographs.

Skiing for Beginners (Scribner's, $4.95), by onetime ski instructor Conrad Brown, is a clear, concise explanation of what is known as the American Ski Technique, a simple learning procedure developed by the Professional Ski Instructors of America. Fine sequence photos amplify the text.

PICKING A SKI AREA

American skiers spend up to $500 million annually for skiing, and, by one estimate, at least, about half that money is wasted. It is a fact that a good percentage of skiers go to the wrong place at the wrong time, and end up paying too much for too little.

If you want value, ski as close to home as possible, a policy that reduces the costly extras of transportation, lodging, and food. Avoid weekend skiing if you are planning to arrange instruction for yourself or a youngster. A child whose first experience at a ski area involves standing in a long lift line is likely to end up as a skater or a bowler. And on weekends you pay premium prices for everything.

If your only available time is on the weekend or other peak period, avoid the "name" resorts, places like Squaw Valley, California; Vail,

Skiing

Colorado; Boyne Mountain, Michigan; or Sugarbush, Vermont. Instead, seek out a less-well-known area. It's not likely to be as crowded and the fees will be less. Remember, when you go to an area that top-flight skiers flock to, it's likely to offer big-mountain skiing, which is hardly necessary for your young novice.

What is said above especially applies to ski areas in the East. Weekends can be a horror. But during the week, it's a different matter. You and your family will pay less for more, much more.

The New York Times Guide to Ski Resorts (The New York Times, $6.95) contains, as the title suggests, appraisals of the nation's ski resorts, evaluating each on the basis of slopes and trails, their number and character, lift fee, accommodations and, important to the parent, the kind and quality of ski instruction offered.

SKI TOURING

Like all other aspects of skiing, ski touring—also known as cross-country—is zooming in popularity. It's an ideal family sport, well suited for children of any age.

It's like hiking on skis. The ski-touring party sets out across farm-land or through forest, over a city park or golf course. Many resorts have set aside special trails for ski-touring enthusiasts. All you have to know how to do is slide one ski forward and then the other, never lifting either from the snow. Poles move alternately with the skis. Anyone can learn the technique in a matter of hours.

Adults in the group often ski ahead to break trail and try out slopes they encounter, all the while keeping a watchful eye on the youngsters. Essentially, each skier sets his own pace.

Cross-country is much less expensive than downhill skiing. For one thing, you never need to buy a lift ticket. And the long, thin wood skis the sport requires cost less. Boots and bindings, much less sophisticated than those used in downhill skiing, are less, too. For example, the Wheel Goods Corporation (2737 Henneepin Ave. South, Minneapolis, Minn. 55408) markets a children's touring package that includes skis, boots, bindings, poles and a wax kit, and the cost is under $60. An adult package is about $90. Write for a catalog.

There are two organizations that will provide you with additional information on cross-country. They are the Ski Touring Council (West Hill Rd., Troy, Vermont 05868), oriented toward the Eastern skier, and the Sierra Club (1050 Mills Tower, 270 Bush St., San Francisco, Calif. 94104), which will give information about ski-touring opportunities in the Rocky Mountain area.

COMPETITIVE SKIING

If your youngster shows more than the usual amount of skiing skill, he may want to ski competitively. Ski clubs and ski areas, plus a handful of snow-country public schools, offer such competition, and the United States Ski Association (1726 Champa St., Suite 300, Denver, Colo. 80202) has a thriving junior program involving youngsters from six through eighteen. Each one of the nine divisions of the USSA sponsors competition for boys and girls in the slalom, giant slalom, downhill racing, cross-country, and jumping. The best skiers in each event are brought together in the annual national championships conducted by the USSA.

If you have any idea that your child might ski competitively one day, it's vital that you obtain the best instruction you can for him right from the beginning. Leading coaches have lamented that many junior competitors have assorted technical shortcomings that retard their progress. It is much easier for a young skier to learn the right way than attempt to unlearn a bad habit that he's developed.

During the late 1950s and early 1960s, when I was an instructor at Mad River Glen, Vermont, I knew Clif Taylor and was familiar with his experiments involving "Shortee Skis." Like many of us, Clif realized that what often made skiing difficult, even awkward, for beginners was the unwieldy length of the skis. "If all you had to do," he said, "was wax the bottom of your shoes, and use the shoes for skis, a person could learn in ten minutes. He could be an 'instant skier.'"

The success of the Taylor-inspired instruction technique can be measured not only in the ever-increasing number of ski areas that offer GLM, but also by the fact that some guarantee results. At Big Vanilla at Davos near Woodridge, New York, the GLM course lasts five and a half days, and if at the end the student still can't ski parallel on a modest slope using skis at least as tall as he is, he's entitled to all the free additional lessons it might take. That's tough to beat.

—Conrad Brown
Author, Skiing for Beginners

RIDING

Riding is one of the most versatile sports there is. The term can refer to hacking a park trail in a pair of bluejeans or a wilderness-country pack trip. It can mean riding to the hounds, horse show competition, rodeo riding or polo.

Riding is something that can be done by a single person or in groups. It can be enjoyed in just about every part of the country at any time of the year. And it's an activity that can provide fun and fitness benefits for one's entire lifetime.

At what age can a youngster learn to ride? Well, it takes a certain amount of strength to be able to control the mount, and it requires coordination, too. The child also has to be mature enough so that he won't be intimidated by the animal. Maybe nine is the right age for your child; maybe ten.

"Age isn't our criterion," says John Franzreb, general manager of Clove Lake Stables in Staten Island, one of the largest pleasure-riding academies in the East. "We can teach just about any boy or girl who knows left from right—and right from wrong." As this implies, a sense of responsibility is required, the understanding that a horse is a thousand-pound, living, breathing, flesh-and-blood creature.

GETTING INSTRUCTION

A child can't learn to ride from reading instruction books (although they are helpful in orienting the beginner) or by getting astride a gentle mount and working things out for himself. Professional instruction—a few supervised lessons, at the very least—are essential.

Inquire among your friends about riding academies in the area. If they are not able to advise you, consult the Yellow Pages (under "Riding Academies"). Visit two or three of them.

The stable doesn't have to be large, nor do the horses have to look like they're being groomed for the Belmont Stakes. The cleanliness of the place is important, however, and bridles, saddles and other pieces of tack should be hung in orderly fashion, not strewn about. As for the horses, they should look well cared for and be bright and alert. Beware of the stable where the animals appear undernourished or have a scrawny look. If you visit a stable in the winter, the horses may have grown their heavy cold-weather coats and thus look shaggy, but this is natural.

All stables that are serious about riding instruction will offer a riding ring, a large circular corral that is used for instruction sessions and practice. Trails for trail riding and bridle paths should be close by.

Styles of riding vary, depending on where you live. In most parts of the East, the English style is taught. Western riding, a style that can be traced to the Spanish conquistadors of the sixteenth century, is the other popular style. But it really doesn't make much difference which one your youngster learns. Simply go along with local custom.

Fees vary, of course, but most academies offer lessons on a "package" basis. A typical package might provide eight 90-minute lessons for $60. Ten one-hour lessons for $55 is another example. These are group lessons, too. They are perfectly adequate as long as the group isn't any bigger than six to ten youngsters.

Often reduced rates are available to schools and camps and to organizations with a particular interest in riding. These include the Boy Scouts, Girl Scouts, 4-H Clubs and Pony Clubs (see below).

When you discuss lessons and fees with the owner or manager of the riding academy, be sure to establish precisely what your youngster is going to learn. You should expect that he will be taught the elementary points (distinctive physical characteristics) of a horse, the parts of the saddle and bridle and something about the care of tack. He should be taught how to approach a horse properly and how to mount and dismount, and he should come to understand the correct

position in the saddle. He should be taught to walk and trot; he should know how to turn and circle. He should learn how to use the seat, legs and hands to increase and decrease pace, and how to rein back. He will be introduced to the canter.

If, after completing the novice course, your son or daughter wants to improve and learn more—perhaps such skills as cantering or riding over fences or ditches—individual lessons will probably be suggested by the riding-academy manager. These can range in price from $10 to $15 an hour.

EQUIPMENT AND APPAREL

For the beginner, the boy or girl who is receiving instruction, very little is required in the way of specialized equipment. Blue jeans are acceptable. While riding boots are not necessary, a sturdy shoe with a well-defined heel is. This rules out loafers and sneakers.

For the rider's safety, a hard-shell riding cap—a helmet—is recommended. The interior should be lined with foam rubber or styrofoam. In addition, the cap should have an adjustable suspension system which holds the shell away from the wearer's head. It should also have a chin strap. Caps cost from $20 to $25.

The serious rider will want jodhpur boots or English riding boots, stretch breeches or jodhpurs, and perhaps a riding coat, vest and gloves. Many equipment dealers provide elaborate catalogs, among them Miller's (123 East 24th St., New York, N.Y. 10010) and Kauffman & Sons (139 East 24th St., New York, N.Y. 10010). Miller's catalog, titled "Everything for Riding," costs $1; Kauffman's catalog is 50¢.

PONY CLUBS

The United States Pony Clubs (Pleasant St., Dover, Mass. 02030) is an organization that you should know about if your youngster plans to become a serious rider. With a membership of about 8,000 boys and girls, it consists of 19 regional groups and 210 local clubs. Its objective is "to encourage young people to ride and to learn to enjoy all kinds of sports concerned with horses and riding." Clubs are also active in training young riders in the proper care of their animals.

Membership is open to any boy or girl under twenty-one. Annual dues are modest, $2 a year per member.

Pony Clubs are especially active in conducting working rallies. At each, instruction is given in such subjects as dressage, cross-country riding, stable management, mounted games, etc. Write for more information about club membership and activities.

The organization also publishes many instructional books and booklets on such topics as horsemanship, care of tack and equipment, care of horses and ponies, riding to hounds, dressage—everything. Write and request a list of publications.

ICE SKATING

The motion of the feet in skating is rather an unusual one. The ankles have to move forward and back but never from side to side. Only in this way is the skater able to use his thigh muscles to create the drive and acceleration required.

As this may imply, it is vital that the youngster's skates fit perfectly. Many instruction books claim it is all right for parents to purchase skates that are a size or two larger than actually needed, the idea being that the youngster will eventually grow into them. But skates that are too big don't give the ankle support a beginner requires, and a child isn't able to control them fully.

The skates you buy should fit the youngster's feet as snugly as the shoes he wears. The best way to economize is to buy at a shop that permits you to trade in used skates, or at least will suggest where they might be traded in. When being fitted, the youngster should wear a thin pair of woolen socks, the same kind he'll be wearing when skating. There's no need to wear two pairs to keep the feet warm, incidentally.

The place where the skater needs maximum support is at the heel. It must fit snugly into the boot's heel pocket. It will if the boot is the right size and laced properly. This means the laces must be pulled tightly at a point beginning just above the instep, or in front of the ankle. This forces the heel back into the heel pocket. If you visit a rink and look at the way the youngsters lace their skates, you will see countless different styles, but it is generally agreed that skates should be laced in herringbone fashion, that is, with the laces crisscrossing.

If you buy quality skates and take the time to get a proper fit, and if the youngster laces them right, he'll never be accused of having "weak ankles." This concept is a myth, in fact. The idea of "weak ankles" dates to the early years of the century, when the skate itself was attached to the wearer's street shoes by means of clamps and straps. With this type of equipment there was nothing to prevent the ankle from bending sideways. With modern skates there is.

For purely recreational skating—that is, not ice hockey or speed skating—buy what are generally known as figure skates. These have

Ice Skating

a blade that is about $1/8$ inch wide; in length it goes slightly beyond the boot. At the blade front, there are a series of sharp points which are used in maneuvering and turning. Because skates of this type lace high on the ankle and have a wider blade than hockey skates, they are considered best for the beginner.

But if your youngster is a hockey fan and wants to play the game, it's not likely you'll be able to get him into a pair of figure skates. Most boys consider them sissyish. The hockey skate has a thinner blade; it measures about $1/16$ inch in width. This permits the wearer to execute the sharper turns and generate the faster speeds that hockey demands. The blade is reinforced with steel tubing.

Hockey boots are reinforced to protect the wearer from being injured by the puck, a swinging stick, or a skate blade. There are steel caps within the toe leather, and there are extra thicknesses of leather along the boot sides. Nylon or wire mesh built into the back of the boot protects the wearer's Achilles tendon. The boot tongue is lined with felt to protect the instep. Some manufacturers now offer special skates for defensemen which have extra padding at the ankles and thicker-than-normal tongues. Many hockey leagues require that skates be equipped with plastic covers over the blade's rear tip. These prevent the blade from stabbing a teammate or opponent.

A pair of quality skates with all the characteristics described above costs about $40. If you pay much less, you will be getting boots of inferior leather that will stretch when they get wet and shrink and harden as they dry out. Reinforcing will be of cardboard. Don't compromise, especially if your youngster is a novice.

Young skaters who plan to do competitive racing should wear the specialized speed skate, which features a particularly long blade, up to 18 inches in length, and which is often as thin as $1/32$ inch. The boots of racing skates are very thin leater and are light in weight.

No matter what type of skates you buy, also purchase a pair of plastic or leather guards that fit over the skate blades. These protect the blades when they are not in use, and a skater can put them on to walk between his locker and the rink.

Encourage your youngster to take care of his skates, wiping dry the boots and blades after each skating session. Rust can form on the blade bottom and dampness can weaken the boot leather.

LEARNING THE FUNDAMENTALS

If you're going to teach your youngster how to skate yourself, don't make the mistake of beginning instruction on the ice. Have him

61

Ice Skating

walk around on the skates first; have him balance on one foot, then on the other. Check to see that he is not going over on his ankles. If he is, the chances are that the skates don't fit properly or they're not laced right.

Have the youngster do a few knee bends, slowly at first, before he goes out onto the ice. By squatting down and rising a few times, he'll begin developing a sense of balance.

The big difference between skating and walking is the glide, and the idea of gliding has to be stressed once you transfer operations to the ice. Give the young skater a few minutes to get used to the feel of things, then encourage him to take a couple of steps, ending the sequence with a glide. Continue the exercise—step, step, glide—until he begins to show discernible progress. Don't be concerned if he doesn't seem to be building up much gliding momentum. Once he's learned the basic motion, speed will come eventually.

It's best if he learns this fundamental without your holding or supporting him in any way. Youngsters don't mind falling down. It doesn't hurt them, especially in the case of toddlers, because they don't have far to fall. Tell the child to try to sit down as he goes down.

Some instructors have their pupils grasp a four-legged chair and push it around the ice. This gets the child into the habit of using the inner edge of the skate blade to drive himself forward. And because he is supported by the chair, he has no fear of falling, or very little.

Little by little, get the youngster to lengthen his strides, with each one blending into the next. While he is pushing off on the inner edge of his left blade, he should be gliding on the right, and the weight of his body should be concentrated over his right leg. Be sure his driving leg comes straight on each stride.

There are several ways to stop. There's the snowplow stop, which is very similar to the snowplow in skiing; there's the so-called T-stop, in which the feet are positioned like the letter T; and there's the hockey stop. In the last, the body turns at right angles to the direction in which the skater is heading.

The snowplow stop is the easiest to learn. As the youngster glides along, have him slide his toes together. The blades will skid sideways, slowing him to a halt.

Dick Button, world figure skating champion from 1948 through 1952 and twice a gold medalist in Olympic competition, is the author of the best book on skating instruction. Titled *Instant Skating* (Grosset & Dunlap, $1.95), it covers not only the fundamentals but such advanced forms as dancing on skates and pair skating. Sequence photos are featured throughout.

Ice Skating

SKATING COMPETITION

Competitive skating can be speed skating or figure skating. In the former, competitors race at various distances around an oval course.

Figure skating is part dancing, part acrobatics. Judges appraise each skater's performance and award points accordingly. The points are averaged and multiplied by a degree-of-difficulty factor. There are required forms, known as school figures, and free skating. The jumps, spins and splits which make up the free skating phase are judged on the basis of skill of execution as well as artistic merit.

Speed skating competition is conducted under the supervision of the various state organizations that make up the Amateur Skating Union of the United States (Route 2, Box 464, Kenosha, Wisc. 63126). Competitive figure skating is the domain of the U.S. Figure Skating Association (178 Tremont St., Boston, Mass. 02111). The USFSA, with more than 25,000 members, establishes rules and appoints officials for meets and determines the amateur status of competitors. Besides the magazine *Skating,* which is issued eight times annually, the organization also publishes a variety of "how-to" booklets, such as "Evaluation of Errors in Figures," "How to Organize and Conduct Competitions," and "Ice Dances." Write for a publication list.

FENCING

Fencing is swordplay, and as such it is a sport of skill, speed and stamina. Don't think of it as something ritualistic or sissyish; don't rate it with bowling or archery or other mild forms of exercise. Fencing is a vigorous sport, requiring balance, deftness and dexterity. Few other sports, probably no other, sharpen hand-eye coordination as does fencing.

Unlike other team sports, fencing "trains the individual as an individual," the late T. F. Windsor, a respected authority, once observed. It's true; besides developing a youngster's coordination and muscle structure, the sport can help to awaken a feeling of individuality and a sense of responsibility.

And fencing has more than the usual amount of carry-over value. A fencer does not attain a competitive peak until he has reached his late twenties or early thirties, and it is not unusual for a top-flight competitor to be in his middle forties. Obviously, experience is an extremely important factor, compensating for loss of speed and increased reaction time.

A youngster's size is no great factor. One recent Olympic medalist was tall and husky, and a ranking U.S. fencer is a slender 5-foot-6.

Fencing

Some boys and girls fence simply because it is a sociable form of exercise. But many others are involved in the sport competitively.

Undoubtedly there is a fencing group in your area. It may be located in a high school, college, community center or YMCA. Large cities have private fencing clubs and schools of fencing. Whenever a fencing group meets, practice sessions are scheduled under the supervision of an amateur or professional coach.

EQUIPMENT AND RULES

There are three different fencing weapons—the foil, the épée and the saber. With all of them the objective is the same: to hit your opponent without being hit yourself.

The foil, the lightest of the weapons, weighs about 17 ounces and is 43 inches long. The tapered blade is more flexible toward the tip and bends easily when contact is made. In competition, the only legal target is your opponent's torso. (Opposing fencers wear metallic vests. When a foil hits the target area, an electrical circuit is completed and the scoring apparatus registers a touch.) Five touches win in men's competition, four in women's.

The épée is the same length as the foil but heavier—up to 27 ounces—and not as whippy. A touch is made with the tip of the weapon and every part of the opponent's body is a valid target. Electrical apparatus aids in judging and scoring. Five touches win. There is no women's competition in épée.

The saber is about the same weight and length as the foil, but has a flat blade. Touches, five of which win, can be scored with the side of the blade as well as the point. The target is the upper body—"any place," say the rules, "above the juncture of the legs and trunk." There is no women's competition.

A bout begins at the center of a 6-foot-wide strip, and touches can be scored only when the fencer is on the strip. The strip for foil is 39 feet long, and that for épée and saber is 46 feet long. If a foilsman retreats off the end of the strip once, or an épéeist or saberman twice, he is penalized one touch, just as if he were hit. In men's competition, bouts for all weapons are six minutes in length; in women's competition, bouts are five minutes.

The standard method of attack is the lunge, with the attacker advancing into striking range by a march—that is, by moving the front foot first, or a jump, which means moving both feet together. He then quickly extends his weapon arm and front leg forward as far and as fast as he can. His opponent attempts to parry by deflecting the blade, and then launches a riposte, a counterattack. The exchange continues until one fencer is hit or until the head official, called the director, halts the match for a loss-of-ground penalty.

This brief description gives no hint of the many, many subtleties involved, nor does it indicate how the basic techniques of the sport are changing. Judges used to place the most emphasis on the sequence of action, on one's overall style. But with the advent of electrical scoring equipment, the fact of the touch, not how it is achieved, is the important thing.

Uniforms and masks. A padded uniform protects the body. If you are planning on buying a uniform, get the type with extra material for letting out the seams. A uniform of this kind, since it can be easily altered, will last for years.

Be aware that there are many types of masks—practice masks, three-weapon masks, electrical masks, etc. The mask should not only protect the front half of the head and neck but it also must fit comfortably. The Castello Fencing Equipment Co. (836 Broadway, New York, N.Y. 10003) is the leading U.S. mask manufacturer, and sells all other fencing equipment. Write for a free catalog.

George Santelli, Inc. (412 Avenue of the Americas, New York, N.Y. 10011) also sells all types of weapons and equipment. On the Pacific Coast, there is Joseph Vince Co. (15316 S. Crenshaw Blvd., Gardena, Calif. 90249) and American Fencer's Supply (2122 Fillmore St., San Francisco, Calif. 94115). All three firms provide free catalogs.

ORGANIZATIONS

The Amateur Fencers League of America (249 Eton Place, Westfield, N.J. 07090) organizes and conducts fencing events on local and national levels. The organization also participates in the selection of teams and individuals to represent the United States in Olympic competition, sponsoring junior Olympic programs and operating Olympic training camps.

The AFLA publishes fencing's rulebook and a bimonthly magazine, *American Fencing.* If you're interested in learning whether there are AFLA members in your area, send your zip code to the organization secretary. He will check it against the AFLA's membership roster. A student membership in the AFLA, for youngsters under age nineteen, is $2.

While experts say that it is just about impossible to learn to fence from a book, there are a number of books available containing fencing instructions. Send a stamped, self-addressed business-size envelope to the secretary of the AFLA for a list of them.

Among those recommended are: *Fencing* (Ronald Press, $5.50), by Hugo and James Castello, and *All About Fencing* (Stanley Paul & Co., $4.50), by Bob Anderson.

BOWLING

It may come as news to you, but bowling is fast becoming the nation's most popular participant sport among young people. Presently, according to the American Junior Bowling Congress, bowling is surpassed only by Little League Baseball in terms of number of participants.

For 1973, membership in the AJBC exceeded 700,000 boys and girls, with two-thirds of that number classified as Bantams, youngsters age twelve or younger. Boys and girls who are age thirteen through fifteen are classed as Juniors, and those age sixteen through twenty-one are seniors. Complete information on the program can be obtained from the AJBC's national headquarters (5301 South 76th St., Glendale, Wisc. 53129).

Just about every bowling center has an AJBC league program. It costs 25¢ for a boy or girl to join. The young bowler receives a membership card, a subscription to *Junior Bowler,* which is published six times a year, and a chance to participate in the organization's huge awards program. It is almost certain that he or she will receive a trophy, emblem, or medal of some type. The AJBC distributes more than 300,-000 awards each year. Of course, the young bowler will also be assessed a weekly fee to cover the cost of games bowled.

Bowling

Should a youngster participate in an AJBC league program, don't be concerned about a loss of athletic eligibility. The program has won the sanction of the National Federation of High School Athletic Associations.

Organized bowling programs are popular among boys and girls because every youngster is a participant. There are no bench-sitters, a claim few other sports can make.

The main disadvantage of bowling is that it cannot be considered a vigorous form of exercise. Like archery or horseshoes, it is rather isotonic in nature. It seldom makes any great demands on one's oxygen-producing process.

GETTING STARTED

Inquire at your local bowling center about the availability of junior bowling instruction. Some centers have a qualified specialist on staff. The word "qualified," in this case, refers to a person who has completed a course of instruction given by the AJBC. Instructors who have won certification can be identified by the special arm patch they wear or certificate they have received—the latter would probably be on display at the bowling center.

Sometimes a parent will hesitate about introducing a youngster to bowling because he believes the boy or girl will be incapable of handling the weight of the bowling ball. This really shouldn't be a problem.

There are two "secrets" in coping with the weight of the ball. One is getting a ball that fits properly and is an appropriate weight for the person bowling; the other has to do with developing a rhythmic delivery, one in which the ball is permitted to swing backward and forward naturally.

Bowling balls for youngsters vary from 9 to 12 pounds in weight, although many teen-age boys and girls, and even preteeners, are able to handle 16-pounders, the maximum weight. The general rule to follow in selecting a ball is to use the heaviest weight possible—the heaviest the child can control. Just keep in mind that high scores in bowling relate to accuracy, not power or speed, so always be willing to sacrifice ball weight for control.

It is not necessary to purchase a ball; in fact, I recommend that you don't. The finger and hand size of a growing boy or girl can change quickly. A ball that is custom-fitted in September is likely to be too small by spring, and can cause finger blisters and even completely discourage the user.

Instead of buying a ball, visit a bowling center and show the youngster how to select a ball that fits properly from the scores of "house balls" available for customer use. Inquire as to whether these balls are color-coded as to weight. For example, in some bowling centers all 16-pounders are solid black, while 12-pounders are black but flecked with yellow. In still other bowling centers, the ball's weight in pounds is etched into the surface near the finger holes.

Bowling

Ball fit is affected by the size of the thumb and finger holes and also by the span, which is the distance between the thumb and finger holes as measured over the ball's contour. The thumb hole should have some roominess to it. Have the youngster insert his thumb, then tell him to rotate it. If he feels just the slightest friction, the fit is right.

The fingers should fit more snugly. Why they should is easy to understand. When the ball is delivered, it's the thumb that comes out first. The fingers—the middle and index fingers—then lift upward, imparting roll. The fit of the fingers must be on the snug side so that you can get sufficient lift as you release.

Once you have found a ball with thumb and finger holes of proper size, check the span. Have the youngster insert his thumb and lay his fingers over the contour of the ball so that they cover the related finger holes. If the span is correct, the knuckles of the fingers should be just beyond the inside edges of the finger holes. Using a ball with too wide a span puts too great a strain on the fingers; too narrow a span causes the bowler to clutch the ball as he delivers. Either way, he can't control the ball properly.

Once a youngster becomes accomplished in the sport and starts bowling frequently with friends or in organized league competition, it's worthwhile to buy a custom ball. By then he'll be knowledgeable about the weight that suits him best. He's also likely to know all about grips. All house balls have what is known as a conventional grip, which means that the holes have been so drilled that the thumb can be inserted to its full length and the fingers inserted almost to their full length. In contrast to the conventional grip is the fingertip grip, which many top-flight bowlers prefer. In this grip, as its name implies, the thumb and fingers are inserted only up to the first joint. This gives greater control as the ball is released, and greater control means increased lift and increased roll, both of which are important in getting the ball to hook. But this isn't a topic that the beginner bowler or you, his instructor, has to be concerned about.

A bowling ball costs from $15 to $25. The more expensive types are made of hard rubber, and the cheaper ones of a plastic material. As a general rule, it's better to make your purchase at a bowling center pro shop rather than a department store or discount center. At the bowling center you have a better chance of being fitted by someone who is informed and experienced in the art—and it is an art. If you purchase a ball and the youngster does outgrow it, don't discard it. Take it to a bowling pro shop and ask to have the holes plugged (with a liquid plastic which hardens) and redrilled. The operation costs about $5. Bowling bags are inexpensive, beginning at about $5.

Bowling shoes are a worthwhile investment. A pair costs about $10. Of course, shoes can be rented for a small fee, usually about 25¢. It is better, however, to own your own for sanitary reasons.

Before your boy or girl begins to bowl, be sure that he or she has a clear understanding of the lane and approach markings. The lane is about 62 feet in length; the approach is 15 feet. The two are separated by the foul line. Embedded in the lane at a point 12 to 16 feet beyond the foul line are seven small, slim triangles. Called rangefinders, they are used in aiming the ball. For example, many bowlers, instead of aiming directly at the pins, seek to roll their ball over the second rangefinder from the right-hand side of the lane. They know that if the ball does this it will continue on a path that brings it into the 1-3 pin pocket, the strike pocket.

Another set of targets is embedded in the lane at a distance of 6 to 8 feet from the foul line. These, made from wooden dowels, are small and circular. Some bowlers prefer these to the triangular rangefinders.

There are three sets of dowels embedded in the approach, each series arranged parallel to the foul line. Bowlers use these dowels to help make their starting and finishing positions correct. To do well in bowling, you have to be consistent—able to deliver the ball in precisely the same way each time. The dowels are meant to help in this regard. As he takes his stance, a bowler might place the toe of his left foot on the center dowel of one of the sets at the end of the approach. He checks to see to it that his left foot is there on every roll. The dowels at the foul line are used in similar fashion—to check the position of the left foot after the ball has been released.

DELIVERING THE BALL

Youngsters should be taught a four-step approach, taking a starting stance about 4½ feet from the foul line. On the first step (with the right foot), the ball is pushed out, down and to the right; on the second step, the ball swings back. It reaches almost shoulder level, the peak of the backswing, on the third step. With the final step, the ball is brought forward and released, with the bowler bending his left knee and sliding on his left foot.

The key to a successful delivery and to coping with the weight

of the ball is the pushaway, the thrusting out of the ball on the first step. If you get the ball swinging on the first step, the problems you have with the rest of the delivery should be minimal.

Young bowlers cause difficulty for themselves by rushing the foul line. They do this in an effort to get as much speed as possible on the ball, believing the greater the speed the more the pins will mix and fall. Rushing the line, however, causes a variety of timing problems. The release of the ball and the left foot's slide must occur simultaneously in order to deliver a ball that is accurate and rolls with authority. You can't coordinate foot and hand action when you rush.

If your youngster is in too much of a hurry, get him to slow down by having him count cadence as he approaches: "One . . . two . . . three . . . four." Emphasize that the approach must be slow and deliberate.

One thing that hampers young bowlers is their concern with how many pins they're able to knock down—or, rather, their *undue* concern. You really can't blame a youngster for wanting to achieve a high score; that's the idea of the game, after all. But at the outset a youngster should concentrate on technique, on developing an effective delivery.

If a youngster gets into a habit of paying too much attention to pinfall, have him "shadow bowl" for a while. Ask the manager to raise the pins or otherwise remove them from the lane and keep only the ball-return mechanism functioning. Professional bowlers often shadow bowl when trying to work out delivery flaws.

> *For a child, bowling is a game of walk and roll, not run and throw. Teach the child to walk slowly toward the foul line and roll the ball slowly.*
>
> *The armswing should be like a clock's pendulum—rod-straight, both back and forward.*
>
> *—Charles F. Hall*
> *Manager, American Junior Bowling Congress*

ARCHERY

It is generally agreed that more people than ever before are golfing, boating, camping and playing tennis. Well, they are also taking up archery in record numbers—young people especially.

Tournament competition is one of the chief appeals of the sport. The National Archery Association of the United States conducts local, state, regional and national matches for archers of all ages and both sexes. This is one sport in which a young boy or girl can outdo his parents or other grown-ups, and on more than one occasion in recent years, U.S. target-shooting champions have been teen-agers, and young teen-agers at that.

Target shooting is only one aspect of the sport. There is also field archery and bowhunting, both of which are enjoying record popularity.

Almost any young child can fire an arrow from a bow, but a boy or girl should be at least eleven or twelve before you can expect much in the way of genuine results. It takes a certain amount of upper-body muscle power to enjoy the sport to its fullest and score well, and most young people don't begin to develop real strength until they're approaching their teens.

Your youngster may get some training in archery at summer camp or in school, but even if he doesn't you shouldn't have any difficulty obtaining instruction. In virtually every city and town there are one or more archery clubs or public ranges. Usually a club will have some members who will be happy to start a youngster on his way.

BUYING EQUIPMENT

It's wise to introduce your child to archery by means of low-priced "learning equipment." This consists of a fiberglass bow, a supply of cedar arrows, and a finger tab, the small, palette-shaped piece of leather that covers and protects the creases of the drawing fingers. The complete set shouldn't cost you any more than $20.

Later, if your child wants to take up archery as a competitive sport or to become a bowhunter, you can buy quality equipment. Try to make your purchases at a shop that offers a tryout range.

Bows. Buy your youngster a laminated recurve bow—that is, one with a gentle reverse curve at each end. These give added power to the draw. Few archers use the straight bow.

Weight is important, but not how much the bow weighs; instead the term refers to "pull" weight, the amount of pounds necessary to draw an arrow to its full length. Each bow is marked with its draw weight. Here is a list of the recommended draw weights for boys and girls of various ages:

Children 6 to 10	10 to 15 pounds
Children 10 to 12	15 to 20 pounds
Teen-age girls	20–30 pounds
Teen-age boys	30–40 pounds

Of course, these are only general recommendations. If your youngster is bigger or stronger than average, he may require a bow of greater weight than suggested above.

In buying a bow, try this test. Have the youngster grasp the bow and extend his arm to its full length, then pull back the bowstring to his face and hold it. Once you've found a bow that he can draw easily, purchase one that is about 5 pounds heavier. This is the rule of thumb that the industry recommends.

Bow length is not a critical factor. For the average thirteen- or fourteen-year-old, a bow of medium height—5 to 5½ feet—is fine. Be sure the handle portion of the bow is comfortable for him to grip.

Before you leave the shop, be certain your youngster is able to string the bow. If it's too tall for him, he won't be able to. Have him try it once or twice. The step-through method is the best way to string

a recurve bow. The upper end of the string is loose; the lower end is looped in place over the lower nock. The archer steps over the bow with his left leg, and places the bow's lower tip across the instep of the right foot. His right hand holds the string. Grasping the bow's upper tip in his left hand, he bends it far enough forward to allow him to slip the loop into place.

Arrows. Know what length arrow your youngster requires. Have him extend his arms out in front of his body to their full length and hold a yardstick between his palms, the end resting on his chest. Read off the distance from his chest to the tip of his fingers. This is the length his arrows should be.

Arrow shafts are made of either wood, fiberglass or aluminum. Those of aluminum, because of their uniformity in weight and stiffness, plus their durability, are used in tournament competition, but they're somewhat expensive, costing about $35 a dozen. Beginners usually use wood arrows because they cost much less, but they should be of good quality. The wood has to be cedar or possibly birch, but not pine. The nock—the notch at the end of the arrow into which the bowstring fits—should be made of molded plastic. Never buy arrows in which the nock is simply a notch cut into the end of the shaft. Quality wood arrows cost about $15 a dozen.

The arrow's feathered portion, known as the fletching, should be mounted in a very precise manner. In a quality arrow, the cock feather —the one that is a different color from the other two—should be at right angles to the bowstring when the arrow is nocked. There's a good reason for this. It ensures that fletching won't brush against the side of the bow as the arrow whisks away.

Examine the arrow's nock carefully. Some have a small molded ridge on one side, on the same side as the cock feather. This enables the archer to nock the arrow correctly by feel.

Some of these may seem like very minor points, but they're not. The arrows the young archer in your family uses have to be perfectly uniform in size and weight and everything else, if he plans to advance beyond the stage of backyard stump shooting. Suppose he's practicing with a target and he aims and hits the bull's-eye. He fires a second time, aiming in exactly the same way, but misses by a wide margin. Immediately he tries to figure out why. Maybe he tightened his grip; maybe he plucked the bowstring. He can't question the arrows; he *must* depend on their uniformity. That's why arrow quality is so vital. Without it, an archer simply can't improve beyond a certain level. He can never become consistent. Every practice session is a waste.

The bowsight. Although the bowsight is a relatively recent invention, it has attained widespread use. In both target and field competition, the archers using bowsights are the archers that win.

A sight takes the form of a reference point of one kind or another that is mounted on the upper limb of the bow just above the grip. It can be adjusted vertically for distance and horizontally for crosswind.

Sights can be simple, consisting of no more than a movable pin or set of crosshairs, but you can also equip your bow with telescopic sights that have precision lenses and big pricetags. Manufacturers claim that a telescopic sight can boost an archer's score by 20 percent or more.

If you take your child to a range for instruction, he'll undoubtedly be trained in the use of a bowsight right from the start. But bowsights are somewhat controversial. Many archers hold that the novice should

learn all there is to know about form and technique before he is introduced to the sight. Certainly, the sight makes every target seem to
be at point-blank range, but sight users concentrate on aiming to such
a degree that they are said to neglect their form. A common problem
is the failure to check the arrowhead as the string is drawn, which can
result in an overdraw or underdraw.

   And sights are far from infallible. They're fine when you're shooting on a range and know the distance to be 20 yards, 30 yards, or
whatever, but most sights require adjusting, and so when the user is

Archery

shooting over a distance that has to be estimated, the value of the sight plummets. "In hunting, a bowsight is useless," says one critic. "How do you get an animal to stand still while you figure out the distance?"

Equipment manufacturers have answers to these arguments. When hunting, the archer knows approximately the type of shot he's going to have; it depends on the kind of game he's after and the terrain. If he estimates that he's going to be shooting at from 30 to 50 yards, he adjusts the sight for 40 yards. When he takes aim and the distance is different, he simply allows for it—which is the same thing a bare-bow hunter does.

As for the criticism that sights are harmful to one's form, one scope maker says this: "Using a sight is the only way to learn. It helps reveal mistakes that result from poor form. The secrecy of accuracy is concentration. It doesn't matter if you have a $4 sight or one that costs $200. If you don't concentrate, you won't hit the target. And the sight helps you to concentrate."

Quivers. The type of quiver to buy depends on the kind of shooting your youngster is going to be doing. Target archery requires a belt or a ground quiver. For hunting or field archery, a shoulder quiver is needed.

Targets and matts. The serious target shooter will use only the regulation four-foot archery target. It is gold in the center (worth 9 points), surrounded by concentric rings of red (7 points), blue (5 points), black (3 points), and white (1 point). Have your youngster record his scores from the first day he begins shooting. His progress is likely to surprise you.

Besides a supply of targets, you will need a matt, the coil of tightly woven grass or straw upon which the target is mounted. Regulation matts are 50 inches in diameter and from 4 to 6 inches thick. A quality matt costs $25 to $30.

You can make a temporary matt by gluing together several thicknesses of corrugated cardboard cut from supermarket cartons. Bales of hay wrapped in burlap make a good backstop. You can also construct a backstop out of nested corrugated boxes, filling the spaces between boxes with fine sand or excelsior.

A catalog offered by the Bear Archery Co. (Rural Route #1, Grayling, Mich. 49738) will give you a comprehensive rundown on archery equipment of all types. The catalog is free.

BOWHUNTING

A hunter armed with a rifle has a distinct advantage over his prey;

the archer doesn't. To be successful, he has to know the habits of the game and know how to stalk, and he must have more than average skill with his weapon. As this may suggest, the excitement of bowhunting is not in the kill but in the chase, for the hunter has to be able to outthink his quarry just to be able to get within shooting distance (25 to 30 yards for the average young shooter).

Then he's confronted with other problems. Once he sights his target, he has to get out into the open and move about in order to be able to aim and draw. And, finally, the sound of the bowstring—the twang—travels almost six times as fast as the arrow does, and it is a sound that is loud enough to frighten all but the very boldest game.

If you are still determined to try, you'll be heartened by the fact that no special equipment is required, or at least virtually none. Any bow can be used. An arrow from a 35-pound bow will have about the same amount of impact as a bullet from a .22-caliber rifle. Blunt tips are usually used for small game, and triangular hunting points for deer and other big game. You should know about flu-flus. On arrows of this type, the fletching consists of untrimmed feathers glued completely about the shaft in a tight spiral. A flu-flu will travel at normal speed for 20 to 30 yards, but then the feathers slow it down, so it can be retrieved easily.

Small game animals are almost impossible to bag unless the archer develops a quick-shot technique. This can be practiced by walking through the woods and picking out different targets—a stump, a low tree branch, a pine cone—and aiming and firing quickly. The technique of leading the target, the way a quarterback throws just ahead of his receiver, also has to be mastered.

There are several things that you and your youngster can do to increase your chances of coming home with something more than tired feet. You can camouflage your bows (camouflage covers can be bought) and also wear clothing that helps you to blend in with the natural surroundings. You can use string silencers, which can be purchased in an equipment store.

A good time to hunt is after a heavy rain. The sodden forest floor enables you to move silently. Or you can conceal yourself behind a blind. Tree blinds are effective, because some game animals never look above eye level. Whether your blind is at ground level or up high, test-shoot the distances to prospective targets.

Calling will help to lure animals close enough for a shot. Commercial game calls, available at hunting and fishing supply stores, are simple to use. All you have to do is follow the instructions that come

Archery

with the call. Actually, you'll probably need two—a long-range call and a close-in call, sometimes called a "squeaker." Raccoons respond well to calls, as do hawks and some owls.

The Archer's Bible (Doubleday, $1.95), by Fred Bear, contains several informative chapters on bowhunting, and there's a chapter on bowfishing, too.

Many states have a bowhunting season, and have set aside special areas for the exclusive use of bowhunters. Contact the fish and game commission in your state to find out the regulations that apply to bowhunting.

CLUBS AND ORGANIZATIONS

Joining an archery club will enhance your youngster's enjoyment of the sport. There are thousands of clubs in operation; surely there is one in your neighborhood. Within a 40-mile radius of New York City, not noted as a hotbed of archery activity, there are more than 150 archery clubs, and each either owns its own shooting range or has access to one.

Clubs that specialize in target archery are affiliated with the National Archery Association of the United States (2833 Lincoln Highway, East Ranks, Penna. 17572). This organization also publishes *Archery World,* a bimonthly magazine, and archery pamphlets and guidebooks.

Field-archery clubs are organized according to the rules of the National Field Archery Association (Route 2, Box 514, Redlands, Calif. 92373). The NFAA publishes *Archery,* a monthly magazine, and *The Handbook of Field Archery,* an annual publication.

Archery clubs usually maintain their own ranges or have use privileges at a local commercial range. While the principal advantage of club membership is that it gives you a place to shoot, clubs also bring you in contact with experienced archers, some of whom are sure to be able to give you good advice on tackle and shooting form.

III AQUATIC SPORTS

SWIMMING AND DIVING
SNORKEL DIVING AND
SCUBA DIVING
WATER SKIING

SWIMMING
AND
DIVING

Swimming, from a standpoint of physical fitness, is one of the best sports there is, matched only in value by running. A swimmer exercises most of the body's large muscle areas, not just those of the arms and legs.

Swimming competition is worldwide, reaching a high point in Olympic years. If you're thinking in terms of competitive swimming for your son or daughter, you'll probably have to move quickly. Swimmers reach a peak of proficiency at a younger age than any other group of athletes. Look at the record book; the champions are mostly teen-agers.

One disadvantage to swimming is that you need a pool. Another— one that applies to young children—is fear of the water. Occasionally a youngster simply doesn't want to learn how to swim. This fear may have resulted from an unhappy experience he once had, like being ducked or thrown into deep water, or he may have heard a horror-filled tale of a drowning or a disaster at sea.

However, the more common reason a child doesn't want to take swimming lessons is the natural disinclination most people have toward doing anything in which they are not skilled. It can apply to skiing or Gaelic football.

89

Find out exactly why your child doesn't want to learn how to swim. If real fear is involved, try introducing him to the water gradually. Take him by the hand and walk with him into water that is about up to his waist. Then take him into water that is chest-deep, then into water that reaches to his chin. Have him jump up and down and do anything else that helps him to relax and feel at ease.

Have him duck his head and exhale underwater. Have him jump from a raft or the pool edge and catch him. Teach him how to do a simple glide float. In water that is about waist-deep, have him push off from a standing position, his arms extended in front of him, his legs back, his face buried in the water. Be sure he keeps his eyes open. He should travel 8 or 10 feet before stopping.

If your child has a deeply rooted fear of the water, don't believe that his fear is going to vanish once he learns how to swim. Many parents do. The fact that a youngster knows how to execute swimming's basic strokes and kicks doesn't mean that he isn't going to continue to be tense in the water. His apprehensions will eventually subside, but it's a gradual process.

TEACHING A CHILD TO SWIM

Most parents have misgivings about teaching their own children how to swim, and are inclined to leave the task to a summer-camp instructor or someone they feel to be professionally qualified. This is true even when the parents are good swimmers themselves.

Yet parents have no valid reason for believing they are unqualified. A couple of points are important, however. One is to set aside a certain time for lessons, and confine instruction to that period and only that period. The length of each lesson should be no more than thirty minutes and the frequency of lessons should be no more than two or three times a week. When the lesson is over, it's over. Don't constantly correct the child as he plays in the water. Don't nag him.

A second point to remember is that the training program should be fun, for both parent and child. Don't criticize every mistake the child makes. Evaluate his performance on a general basis, according to his age and experience.

There are many types of swimming aids available that can be used to help get a child used to the water. These aids help the novice to float higher in the water and thereby make it easier for him to breathe. Difficulty in breathing is what discourages most youngsters. Once this problem is solved, the child can concentrate on arm strokes and leg kicks.

The most popular swimming aids are belts, buoys, or rings which go about the swimmer's waist or chest. Avoid the kinds made of foam rubber or styrofoam; it's better to purchase the inflatable type. An inflatable belt, buoy, or ring will allow you gradually to decrease the amount of air as the youngster's skill increases and his confidence builds.

At the beginning, adjust the amount of air in the device so the youngster's body floats, to use an instructor's term, "comfortably low" in the water. This means that his shoulders should be beneath the water's surface as he strokes, while his chin should be at about the same level as the surface. Instruct him to keep his mouth open as he breathes.

A kickboard is another helpful aid for the novice. Using a kickboard not only helps a youngster overcome his uneasiness, but also can be extremely valuable in teaching how to kick efficiently. Kickboards of styrofoam are available everywhere, even in large drugstores, and they're more than adequate. They're also inexpensive. The child's first use of a kickboard, or any swimming aid for that matter, should be restricted to water that is about waist-deep.

During these early stages, a child can also be taught to use a stationary support, a dock or the edge of a pool or raft, in learning how to kick. While face down, have him grasp the edge while placing one hand below the surface and the other above it. This gives him the support he needs to straighten his body and legs. Instruct him to keep his shoulders beneath the surface, to tilt his head back, and to keep his mouth open for breathing.

He can also use a dock or pool edge while in a back-down position, reaching over his shoulders to grasp the edge. He then extends his legs and kicks. The back of his head rests against the edge.

Of course, swimming aids are not absolutely necessary, and more than a few instructors feel they can retard a child's development. Sometimes a child does become too dependent on the buoy or kickboard, or whatever, and does not feel secure in the water without it.

If you plan to hire an instructor to teach your child how to swim, arrange to pay him for achieving a specific goal, not merely for a certain number of lessons. If the instructor says, "I'll teach the child how to swim," have him define exactly what he means. Your child, when he has completed the course, should be able to jump into the water, swim several yards, turn around, and return.

The American National Red Cross offers several swimming and water-safety courses, and they're not just for beginners. Courses for advanced swimmers teach different swimming styles and build the pupil's endurance. For information, call your local Red Cross chapter.

DROWNPROOFING

If your child enjoys water sports (and even if he doesn't), it's a good idea to have him "drownproofed." This means he'll be taught a set of simple skills which he can use to keep himself alive in deep water should he be confronted by an emergency, like a cramp or accidental injury.

Drownproofing was originated by Fred Lanoue during a period in the 1950s when he was the swimming coach at the Georgia Institute of Technology in Atlanta. Later he was hired by the Peace Corps to teach drownproofing to its volunteers, and he has served on national committees of the Red Cross, YMCA and Boy Scouts of America.

Drownproofing is based on one's ability to float in the water, but not float horizontally in the commonly accepted manner. To Lanoue, floating means being almost vertical in the water, with only the top of the floater's head ever getting above the surface. From this, what is called a basic "resting" position, the swimmer executes a scissors kick and presses his outstretched arms toward his sides. This action brings his head far enough out of the water to enable him to exhale and inhale. He then allows his body—still vertical—to slip beneath the surface for another "rest period." In beginners, the period of rest is about three seconds, but they can quickly increase it to ten seconds and even more.

Lanoue used to lecture to civic groups on the merits of drownproofing. Often there would be a swimming pool close at hand. Before he began, Lanoue would introduce a group of boys and girls, no more than four or five years old, each of whom had been drownproofed. Some of the children would have their ankles tied together, others their hands. Into the pool they would go as Lanoue began his lecture, and they would remain there until he finished, usually about thirty-five minutes. Lanoue's ten-year-old daughter had been so thoroughly drownproofed that she could stay afloat for as long as eight hours in a crowded swimming pool.

Lanoue explains drownproofing in detail in his book *Drownproofing, a New Technique for Water Safety* (Prentice-Hall, $3.95). The volume also contains interesting chapters on other aspects of swimming, such as overcoming the fear of water, and techniques for underwater swimming and for traveling long distances without tiring.

COMPETITIVE SWIMMING

Swimming records seldom last more than a year or two, thanks to improved training methods, better diets and the continual refinement of swimming techniques. Another factor is the vast swimming program for children developed and administered by the AAU. It involves children of all ages.

There is no clearly defined swimming "season"; it's a year-round activity. Women compete under the same rules as men, although not against them, at least not as of 1973.

These are the basic strokes used in competitive swimming:

Crawl.   The fastest stroke, the crawl is used in free-style racing. The swimmer is face down; the arms are brought alternately over the water and pulled toward the thighs. The feet move alternately in a flutter kick.

Backstroke.   The swimmer is face up; his arms stroke alternately. He uses a flutter kick.

Breaststroke.   From a face-down position, the swimmer moves his arms simultaneously forward and out. His shoulders are at the level of the water's surface. Both legs kick together in a froglike motion. All leg action is below the surface.

Butterfly stroke.   A variation of the breaststroke, the butterfly has been used in competition since 1954. The arms move forward quickly and together; the pull is to the thigh (not to the chest, as in the breaststroke). The legs move in a synchronized up-and-down motion called a "dolphin kick."

The standard events for boys and girls age ten and under include the following:

94

Swimming and Diving

Short Course	*Long Course*
(20 or 25 yards, 25 meters)	(50 or 55 yards, 50 meters)
50 yards freestyle	50 meters freestyle
100 yards freestyle	100 meters freestyle
200 yards freestyle	200 meters freestyle
50 yards backstroke	50 meters backstroke
50 yards breaststroke	50 meters breaststroke
50 yards butterfly	50 meters butterfly

In addition, there are medleys and relays. In an individual relay, the same swimmer uses four strokes in turn—breast, butterfly, back and crawl—over a 100-yard or 200-yard (or 200-meter) course. Medley relays involve four members of a team, each using a different stroke. The usual distance is 200 yards (or 200 meters).

For more information about competitive swimming, write to the AAU (3400 West 86th St., Indianapolis, Ind. 46268). Ask for a copy of the *Swimming Rules Manual,* which costs $1. It contains the rules for both age-group and junior Olympic competition, plus the current records for each.

DIVING

Springboard diving is one sport where skilled instruction is vital. Until the young diver acquires a "feel" as to how his body is positioned in the air, he must rely on a coach or instructor for this information.

A novice also needs the aid of an experienced diver to give him advice on the diving board. At the beginning, he should limit his practice to the "low board," the standard 1-meter board. By adjusting the board fulcrum, he changes the balance of the board so that it suits his weight and the particular dive he plans to try. The board should be so installed that when he springs upward, it propels the diver outward slightly, away from the board end.

Safety specialists say that at least 10 feet of water is necessary for practice diving. Water to this depth should extend at least 5 feet in back of the board end, 10 feet in front of it, and 8 feet to either side.

The first attempts from the board should not be dives in the classic sense, but merely exercises meant to develop control and lift. The standing front jump is typical. The diver takes a standing position at the board's front end, bends his knees and springs into the air, entering the water feet first.

96

Swimming and Diving

Competitive diving. Diving competition is conducted from several different height levels: a springboard 1 meter above water level; a springboard 3 meters above water level (the high board); and a platform 5, 7½ or 10 meters above water level.

There are five groups of dives: front dives, back dives, reverse dives (formerly known as gainers), inward dives and twisting dives. Many dives in each of these categories can be performed in three different positions: in the *tuck,* the body is bunched into a ball, the diver bending at the waist and knees; in the *pike,* the body is in the jackknife position, with the waist bent and knees straight; and in the *layout,* the body is fully extended, often with the back arched.

Judges evaluate each dive, rating it on a point scale from 0 to 10. The score of each dive is then multiplied by the degree-of-difficulty factor, which is given in the rulebook. It can range from 1.2 to 3.0.

In high school competition, each diver makes five "required" dives, that is, one from each of the above listed categories, and six optional dives. The score is figured for each, then added. The highest total wins.

Diving Rules, available from the AAU (see address above), gives a comprehensive rundown on competitive diving. The handbook costs $1.

SNORKEL DIVING
AND
SCUBA DIVING

Young people today are well aware of the solitude and spectacular beauty to be found below the surface of the water amidst what Jacques Cousteau has called "the silent world." It was Cousteau himself who triggered the growth in underwater diving as a leisure-time activity when, as a French naval officer in the mid-1940s, he helped develop a workable scuba system, which he called the aqualung.

Not all underwater diving requires air tanks, a regulator and the related equipment. It can be merely snorkel diving. Here the diver is equipped with only a mask, a breathing tube (the snorkel) and a pair of fins. The snorkel diver can swim for extended periods with his head below the surface or, after filling his lungs with air, can dart below the surface for a brief look around.

Either type of underwater diving demands a knowledge of the physics involved, an understanding of pressure and its effect upon the body. A young diver shouldn't be permitted to enter the water until he is well schooled in this subject. The paragraphs that follow cover only the highlights. Entire books have been written on the subject, and these can be helpful, but the only way to become fully informed is by means of a course of instruction, as discussed later in this section.

Snorkel Diving and Scuba Diving

Everyone on earth feels pressure from the weight of the air above him. Since air surrounds the earth to a height of approximately 7 miles, every person has a stack of air 7 miles tall pressing down on him. At sea level this column of air exerts a pressure of 14.7 pounds per square inch (psi).

When a diver enters the water and goes below the surface, he also feels the effects of water pressure. Salt water in the Atlantic Ocean, which weighs approximately 64 pounds per cubic foot, exerts a pressure of .445 psi for every foot of depth. At a depth of 33 feet, the water pressure is 14.7. The absolute pressure at that depth is 29.4 psi, the total of the water pressure plus the air pressure.

The snorkel diver begins to perceive the increased pressure, or, more precisely, the differences in pressure, at a depth of 6 or 7 feet, but it causes him no great difficulty. Air in his lungs is compressed by the increasing pressure the water exerts on his chest cavity, but he hardly notices it. He feels what is called a mask squeeze, which is caused by the mask skirt being pressed tightly to his face. By exhaling into the mask he equalizes the pressure on either side of the faceplate and the pain subsides.

As he goes deeper, he may experience some ear pain. This is caused when air at surface pressure is trapped within the middle ear. Because this air is lower in pressure than the ambient pressure, a differential is produced across the eardrum, the membrane separating the two. The lower the diver descends, the greater the difference in pressure and the sharper the pain.

The solution is to equalize the pressure by introducing air at ambient pressure from the throat through the eustachian tube into the middle ear. Sometimes the diver has to help the air along by swallowing, yawning, or moving his jaw from one side to the other. Another ploy is to hold one's nose, pinch it, and then attempt to blow through it. Divers refer to this as "popping the ears." Sinus cavities within the diver's head are also subject to the pressure differential, but these usually equalize naturally without any effort on the diver's part.

These paragraphs suggest why a person must forego diving when suffering from a cold, hay fever, or any other infection which causes swelling in the sinus membranes or ear passages. When the passages are in such a state, air cannot flow freely, and the resulting buildup of pressure can rupture an eardrum or cause hemorrhaging in tissues lining the sinuses. It also implies why divers never wear earplugs. Not only do they seal off the outer ear and prevent the diver from equalizing

99

pressure, but they can also create a low-pressure pocket between the earplug itself and the eardrum. An eardrum rupture can be the result.

EQUIPMENT FOR SNORKEL DIVING

Buy the mask first; it's vital that it fit the face snugly yet comfortably. Try different shapes. To assure proper fit, have the youngster place the mask over the eyes and nose. Holding it in place with his hand, have him inhale through his nose, then remove the hand doing the holding. The mask skirt should form a seal so tight that the suction created keeps the mask from falling off.

Besides providing an airtight seal, the skirt should be soft and pliable. Inexpensive masks are rigid in construction and can cause discomfort by pressing into the cheeks.

The adjustable strap that holds the mask in place should be a divided band, not merely a single strap. The lens should be of shatterproof safety glass, not plastic. Plastic scratches and also fogs more readily than glass.

Of course, all masks enclose the nose, but in some the nose fits into a small pocket, which permits the wearer to pinch the nose through the pocket material—usually neoprene—when equalizing air pressure. Other masks have built-in purge valves. The idea of the purge valve is to aid in ridding the mask of water which may collect inside. You simply hold the mask tight to your face, and blow briskly through your nose. Water is then forced out through the purge valve.

Newer masks have a wrap-around feature. Small lenses mounted at right angles to the main lens give the wearer a 180° field of vision. With conventional masks, your field of vision is restricted, almost as if you were wearing blinders.

Masks are not expensive. A quality mask of wrap-around style, complete with a nose pocket and purge valve, carries a list price of about $20, and can probably be purchased for 20 to 30 percent below that figure.

The snorkel. When buying a snorkel, get a simple one. All that's needed is a basic J-shaped tube of rubber or neoprene, 12 to 14 inches in length. A snorkel that is any longer than 14 inches is impractical. One that is 20 inches long, say, permits the diver to go only a few inches deeper, but because his chest is subjected to increased water pressure he is unable to fill his lungs with air. So the extra few inches of depth he gets is an advantage that is canceled out by overall lack of efficiency.

100

Snorkel Diving and Scuba Diving

Some snorkels fit between the lips and teeth. With others, you bite the mouthpiece—that is, they fit in between the teeth. Either type is acceptable; it's a matter of wearer preference. Just be sure the mouthpiece is soft and smooth so it will not chafe, and that the flange is big enough to form a tight closure about the lips. Some snorkels have mouthpieces which are fitted with purge valves, but more divers consider this feature of dubious value.

There are several kinds of gimmicks available that are supposed to keep water out of the tube. In one, a small cork ball floats in place to close off the tube end when it becomes submerged. Such accessories should be avoided. They sometimes interrupt the flow of air unexpectedly. For example, the wearer may be preparing to dive and is about to take a deep breath, when suddenly a wave breaks over the tube end, shutting off the air supply. That can be a scary experience for a young diver.

The only accessory that is really necessary is a small rubber tab that holds the snorkel to the mask. Some divers prefer to keep the tube in place by sliding it under the mask strap, but doing this can spoil the airtight seal. Using the small tab is the better method.

The first snorkels were reeds or hollow stalks. The breathing tube you purchase should have the same simplicity as these early models. Plan to pay about $4 for it.

Fins. Fins are available in such a wide array of shapes and sizes that it is difficult to make an intelligent choice. Begin with the matter of fit and you'll make your task easier, because many companies do not make fins in junior sizes. Some fins are equipped with adjustable heel straps and are intended to fit any size foot, but no diver can really expect to get a snug fit with a fin of this kind. Fins with a slipper heel are better. They come in graduated sizes; each graduation is the equivalent of two shoe sizes.

Once you have a properly fitting pair of fins, the other considerations are quite secondary. Usually the blade area is proportional to the fin size. Just be sure that you don't buy a style in which the blade is so wide or stiff that your youngster will have to have legs like a Russian hammer thrower to make himself go. Not only should the blades be of somewhat modest size and weight, but they should have some "whip"; otherwise, the fins can cause foot or leg cramps. Keep in mind that the speed and efficiency with which a diver moves through the water is related to how the fins fit and how well he can control them.

One other word regarding fins. Some have the ability to float. Drop one from a boat or pier and you can easily pluck it out of the water. It seems likely a worthwhile feature, but it's really not. Because of their buoyancy, fins of this type are more difficult to kick with than the conventional kind, especially when young legs are doing the kicking.

Fins range in price from $7.50 to $20. Those toward the upper end of the scale are more for adult-size feet and legs, and their higher price is related to design and construction features which are meant to reduce water drag and increase propulsion. The young beginner need not be overly concerned about such features.

USING SNORKEL EQUIPMENT

You can teach your son or daughter how to use a mask, snorkel and fins in shallow water depths—up to 10 or 12 feet. This is presupposing, of course, that the youngster is a skilled swimmer. But for anything more ambitious than 10 or 12 feet of water, a boy or girl requires special training. Fortunately, courses of instruction are offered in just about every community. How and where to obtain such instruction is discussed below.

To introduce a child to mask, snorkel and fins, use a swimming pool, indoors or outdoors. Teach him how to use the mask first. He should don it by holding the skirt against his face, then looping the strap over the back of his head. (If he puts the strap over his head first, some strands of hair are likely to slip between the skirt and his forehead and spoil the seal.)

He should be taught how to prevent the mask from fogging, how to maintain proper pressure, and how to clear it. Defogging is easy. Dive shops sell a fogging preventative—glycerin, actually—but few divers buy it. Instead, they rub the lens with a raw potato slice before a dive. The more frequently used method is to coat the lens with saliva, then rinse.

Maintaining proper pressure is almost as simple. When the diver goes to the bottom of the pool, he'll notice that the mask presses tightly to his face because of water pressure. All he has to do is exhale slowly through his nose to restore the pressure balance.

To learn to clear the mask, the diver should first practice in shallow water. If the mask has a purge valve, he should experiment in its use. If the mask doesn't, no problem. He can do what most divers do, which is clear the mask when performing a horizontal roll.

While moving through the water on a horizontal plane, the diver places the palm of his right hand on the right side of the lens rim, and presses firmly so that the seal becomes tighter on that side. While

Snorkel Diving and Scuba Diving

exhaling slowly into the mask, he dips his left shoulder and begins to roll. As his head turns, the water collects on the left side of the mask. Since the seal is not as tight on that side, it is forced out by the pressure of the exhaled air. A full 180° turn should completely clear the mask.

Some masks, because of the way they fit on the face, clear more effectively with a vertical tilt. While on a vertical plane—perhaps standing—the diver presses the upper portion of the mask to his forehead. As he tilts his head back, he exhales into the mask, which forces the water out from the mask bottom.

It's important for a young diver to develop confidence in the use of the snorkel—to be aware that even though the tube portion fills, water will not enter his mouth unless he inhales. To clear the tube of water is simply a matter of sending a quick, forceful puff of air into the tube. Not all the air in one's lungs should go into the effort, because a second puff may be necessary to complete the clearing.

Have the young diver experiment with the fins before using them in open water. While holding onto the side of the pool, have him kick, using each leg alternately. What's important is that he use the muscles of the upper leg—the thigh—as well as those of the calf. Each kick must be slow and rhythmic.

Check to see that he bends his leg slightly at the knee as he kicks. The knee should lead the kick on each downswing. The toes should point straight back. There should be some looseness in the ankle, so that the fin blade angles back and sweeps downward with maximum efficiency. Each kick, from beginning to end, should be about the same length as one of the child's normal walking steps.

It's important that the fins never break above the water's surface. Doing so dissipates the power of the stroke (and the noise of the splashing frightens away marine life).

When the young diver transfers to open water, he should keep his arms at his sides as he kicks, his hands touching his thighs. The idea, of course, is to reduce drag.

GETTING SCUBA INSTRUCTION

Before you consider signing up a youngster for instruction in the use of scuba equipment, be sure that he or she is physically qualified for the sport. A thorough examination by your family physician is a must. The prospective diver has to be free of cardiovascular or respiratory disease, and the ear and sinus passages must be capable of equalizing pressure rapidly. Discuss immunization treatments with the examining physician. Inoculations for tetanus and typhoid fever may be in order.

Emotional stability is another requisite. A boy or girl who might possibly panic in making what the Underwater Society of America calls a "life decision" cannot be considered a diving candidate. Some instructors won't accept as pupils boys and girls younger than eighteen.

Several organizations certify scuba instructors: the National Association of Underwater Instructors (NAUI), the oldest and largest of the certifying organizations; the National Association of Skin Diving Schools (NASDS); the National Council of YMCAs; and the Professional Association of Diving Instructors (PADI). Try to select an instructor who has won either NAUI or NASDS certification. The YMCA and PADI certification programs are said to vary in merit from region to region.

104

When a person is instructed by an NAUI-trained teacher, he is likely to find that the course emphasizes the safety aspects of diving. "It's a very physical course," says one instructor. "A person is really tested." The NASDS instructor, on the other hand, is likely to put stress on the recreational aspects of diving. He is, of course, concerned with safe diving, but usually has a more emancipated attitude toward the sport.

A good way to obtain instruction is through a local equipment dealer, the so-called dive shop. Look in the Yellow Pages of the telephone directory in your area. Many of the directory listings carry information as to instruction services and facilities.

Dive shops frequently offer the NASDS course. It usually involves a total of twenty-six hours of instruction, with approximately one-third of the time devoted to lecture periods and two-thirds to pool instruction. The course costs about $50. A handful of dive shops have their own pools, but most depend on the facilities of a local YMCA, Boys' Club, high school or college. Besides lectures and pool instruction, be sure to establish that the course includes an "open-water checkout," that is, use of the equipment in an authentic diving situation, the ocean or a lake.

The National Council of YMCAs is particularly active in scuba instruction and has been since the mid-1950s. Many YMCA instructors have earned NAUI certification.

Inquire at your local YMCA to find out whether there is a course of instruction available. The youngster you're seeking to enroll must be at least seventeen years old. In addition, the boy or girl, without benefit of fins, snorkel or other skin-diving equipment, should be able to tread water for three minutes using only the feet; swim 300 yards; tow an inert swimmer 40 yards; stay afloat for fifteen minutes; and swim underwater for a distance of 15 yards without employing a pushoff.

The cost of the course varies, but in most areas it doesn't exceed $50, and it can be as little as $25. A student has to provide his own mask, fins and snorkel, but the basic scuba equipment—the air cylinder, filler valve and regulator—are usually available at no charge.

The course of instruction is often an excellent one, and the boy or girl who completes it comes away with a clear understanding of how to use scuba equipment as well as a knowledge of the various safety measures involved. In most cases, the course involves twelve instruction sessions, each consisting of a 75-minute lecture and a 90-minute pool period. A course "graduate" is able to:

1. Retrieve mask, fins and snorkel from deep water and don them; clear mask underwater; clear snorkel with face submerged.
2. Swim half a mile with mask, fins and snorkel in less than 20 minutes.
3. Don mask, fins, snorkel and scuba gear in deep water; buddy-breathe; remove equipment.
4. Swim 300 yards on the surface while wearing scuba gear, breathing through snorkel or scuba mouthpiece.

107

5. Tow an inert swimmer 100 yards while wearing scuba gear and breathing through scuba mouthpiece.
6. Lift an individual from deep water to pool deck and apply mouth-to-mouth resuscitation.

The textbook for the YMCA training program, titled *The New Science of Skin and Scuba Diving,* was prepared by a panel of experts representing the Council for National Cooperation in Aquatics. Although some of the material it contains is quite technical in nature, it features several chapters on the basics of skin and scuba diving, first aid for diving accidents, marine life and other topics of general interest. The manual costs $2.75. To obtain a copy, write: National Council of YMCAs, 291 Broadway, New York, N.Y. 10007.

SCUBA EQUIPMENT

The regulator—the automatic device that controls the flow of air from the tanks strapped on the diver's back and adjusts to the ambient water pressure—is the most important piece of equipment a diver owns. When the young diver in your family wants to buy a regulator of his own, it's a good idea to accompany him on the shopping trip.

What makes the selection process difficult is the variety. The nine major manufacturers of diving equipment offer more than forty different regulator models. If you don't get confused, you're the exception.

First of all, keep in mind that there are two principal types—double-hose and single-hose. The star of the old "Sea Hunt" television series always used the two-hose type. The single-hose regulator is the more modern, more popular type.

Both the two-hose and single-hose regulators are of the double-stage type. In the first stage the raw air from the tank is reduced to about 100 psi; it is then fed to the second stage, where it is reduced to the pressure of the surrounding water. (There are also two-hose regulators of a single-stage variety, but these aren't recommended. All single-hose regulators are double-stage.)

In the two-hose regulators, both stages are contained in a metal case that attaches to the tank valve. One hose leads from the case to the diver's mouthpiece, providing him with whatever air he demands. The second hose carries the carbon dioxide he exhales into his mouthpiece to the metal case, where it is expelled into the water.

In the single-hose regulator, one reduction stage takes place at the tank valve, the other within the mouthpiece. A slim hose connects the two. The diver's exhalations are expelled at the mouthpiece.

108

Snorkel Diving and Scuba Diving

Basically, the choice comes down to single-hose or double-hose. Each type has its advantages, but the single-hose has more of them. It's simpler to maintain; there are fewer parts to worry about. And even when the unit does require maintenance or overhaul, the work usually costs less than it does with the more complicated two-hose type.

As far as in-the-water use is concerned, it's something of a tossup. Single-hose regulators are easier to inhale with, two-hose regulators easier to exhale with. Of course, you never really know how the regulator is going to work in deep water. Trying it out in the dive shop is hardly a valid test, and even using it in a pool doesn't give a true reading. One equipment manufacturer makes a point of this in his advertisements, which declare, "See us at 200 feet; we'll show you the difference."

No matter the type you finally choose, the system should include a post for the attachment of a gauge for measuring tank air pressure, a safety device that is now considered mandatory.

How much you pay for the regulator depends to some extent on how much use it's going to get. For a young man who plans only three or four days of diving a year, a regulator in the $60–$80 price range will probably do. The boy who is planning weekly dives will require a more expensive model. Regulators range in price up to $200, the price that professional divers pay.

Besides the regulator, the young diver is also going to need an air tank (a "junior-size" tank costs about $65), a pack frame to hold it to his back ($15), a life vest ($10–$20), and perhaps a compressed-air speargun ($20–$40), an underwater knife ($10–$20), a depth gauge ($10–$40), an underwater light ($10–$35), and, eventually, a round-trip airline ticket to some barrier reef or at least the Florida Keys. The equipment list goes on and on. But the regulator is what is critical; that's where to focus your attention.

Wet suit. When the water temperature gets below 65°, the diver needs protective clothing in the form of a wet suit. Made of foam neoprene and covered with a smooth rubber or nylon skin, it is called a wet suit because it permits a small amount of water to enter and form an insulating layer between the diver's skin and the suit's inner surface.

Suits are manufactured by all leading equipment companies. A jacket and pants are usually all that are necessary, but you can also purchase boots, gloves and other accessories.

A two-piece suit of quality material costs about $85. The price varies somewhat in proportion to the thickness of the neoprene; the more expensive suits are ⅜ or ¼ inch thick.

SKIN DIVING CLUBS

The best way for a young person to become more knowledgeable about local diving opportunities is by joining a diving club. There are hundreds of such clubs in operation. Most are affiliated with a regional or state diving council, and the councils, in turn, form the Underwater Society of America (Ambler, Penna. 19002). Inquire at a local dive shop about club activity. If your YMCA has a diving program, ask there.

Clubs range in size from just a few members to a hundred and more. The members plan dives together. They may charter a boat and go wreck diving; they may plan a Caribbean diving vacation. Clubs often sponsor contests in spearfishing and underwater photography.

WATER SKIING

As the use of fast, maneuverable boats has zoomed in popularity, so, too, has the sport of water skiing. It's an easy sport to learn, and about the only requisites are the ability to swim and the desire to be taught. Boys and girls as young as seven or eight can be schooled in the sport's fundamentals. And learning is always fun.

If you are a skilled water skier, you can probably teach your child the basic techniques. If not, find out whether there is a water-ski school in your area. A qualified instructor should be able to teach your child to ski in just a few lessons. There are hundreds of water-ski clubs operating in the coastal and lake regions of the country, and many of these offer training for beginners. In addition, some equipment dealers have instruction courses available.

TEACHING YOUR CHILD TO SKI

Start every instruction session by having the youngster don a ski vest. These are made of soft, pliable foam and are designed to provide for chest-up, head-back flotation. While vests are available in two or three different sizes, the type you select should have adjustable belts that encircle the chest and waist areas. These assure a perfect fit.

111

Bright yellow is the best color; it offers the highest visibility. Be sure the vest has earned Coast Guard approval. Such vests cost from $25 to $30. Don't attempt to economize by equipping the child with a ski belt. They don't offer nearly the protection.

Check the site carefully before instruction begins. A sandy beach and firm bottom are ideal. The water should be at least 4 feet deep (5 feet for adults) in the instruction area. The surface must be calm, which means the water has to be free of boat traffic. The choppiness caused by other powerboats makes instruction impossible. Never instruct near swimmers.

Begin by showing your youngster how to put on the skis properly. (Have him wet his feet first. Often a ski that seems to fit snugly on a dry foot will work loose in the water.) Holding the heel unit to one side, he should slide his foot into the toe unit as far as it will go. Raising his heel slightly, he should then pull the heel rubber over the back of his foot. Have him use both hands when he does this; otherwise, the ski can go on twisted.

A ski that has been correctly fitted will feel like a tennis shoe that has been snugly laced. If the child has a small foot and you can't adjust the heel unit so as to get a snug fit, have him don a pair of socks.

Learning how to water ski is something like learning how to ride a bicycle. Once the beginner knows how to get started, he's mastered the most difficult part.

Begin your instruction on shore. Drill the child on the safety aspects of the sport first. Have him don a personal flotation device; explain its importance and use. If he falls, either when starting or when skiing, he should let go of the tow bar immediately and raise both hands above his head, clasping them together, a signal that he is all right.

Remind him to watch the rope as it uncoils at the start to be sure there are no loops beneath the surface in which he could become entangled. If possible, there should be three people in the instruction crew besides the skier—the boat operator, an observer who rides in the boat and handles the uncoiling of the rope and generally keeps an eye on proceedings, and the instructor, who skis beside the pupil.

Spend several minutes on dry land simulating water starts. Have the youngster don the skis (and his personal flotation gear), grasp the handle, and squat down. Stand facing him at a point just in front of his ski tips and take hold of the tow line. As you begin pulling, the youngster should rise gradually, keeping his feet flat to the skis. This is vital; if he rises on his toes when making a real start, his heels are likely to come out of the bindings, the tips of his skis will come up,

and a spill will result. His hands should be far enough apart so that his elbows are outside his knees.

Watch to see that he keeps his arms straight as he comes erect. Bent elbows, common among beginners, are an indication that the skier is attempting to pull himself up, which is wrong. He must learn to rise naturally, using his legs to do the work. Check the position of his back, too. It should be straight from start to finish.

Once standing, he should keep his knees flexed slightly in order to maintain his balance. You can judge whether his stance is right by letting go of the line suddenly. If he topples backward, he is obviously off balance. Have him adjust his stance so his weight is concentrated over the bindings.

Explain that when he attempts to start in the water, the position of his body will be the same, except that everything will be tilted back-

113

ward slightly. As the pull begins, his ski tips will come out of the water and he'll be leaning back. Again he should keep his arms straight and his back straight, and let his legs do the work as he rises.

Once operations are transferred to the water, the best way to teach is to have an instructor ski beside the child, using a tow line the same length as the pupil's. The instructor can then handle the signals to the boat operator, telling him when to accelerate and when to slow down, and he can tell the youngster when to begin standing.

At the start, the instructor should take a position right beside the pupil, holding the youngster's arm to help him get his balance. As the boat accelerates, the instructor rises, and by exerting pressure on the child's arm helps him to rise. Once the student begins skiing, the instructor can release his grasp, but he should stay alert to correct the youngster should he do something wrong.

114

Water Skiing

If the pupil falls, the instructor should drop in the water with him. This is mostly to reassure him, but it's also to help get him started again.

With most beginners it takes five or six tries before they are able to get up. However, a very well-coordinated youngster may be able to do it the first time. Once the child has learned to get up, the instructor should allow him to ski for a short time, then have him drop in the water and start again. After three or four successful starts, the youngster need no longer be considered a novice.

SKIS AND OTHER EQUIPMENT

Manufacturers offer skis in a number of "junior" sizes. For the small child, up to ten years of age, pick out skis that are from 4 to 5 feet in length. These, being shorter than the normal ski, are easier to control.

Older children can learn on skis of conventional length, 5-foot-6 to 5-foot-9. While skis that are longer and wider give better support

at slower speeds, they can be awkward to handle when starting because of their greater buoyancy.

Check the bindings and the fins. The two-piece bindings should
be neoprene or a vinyl material; the former is better than the latter.
The toe unit, which encloses the forward part of the foot to the ankle,
is stationary, while the heel unit is adjustable, sliding back and forth
on a plastic or metal track; it clamps in place so that the heel piece
fits snugly to the back of the foot.

The fins are meant to provide stability and prevent skidding on
turns. Check each fin by standing the ski upright and flexing it slightly.
Beware of skis where the leading edge of the fin tends to separate
from the ski bottom. These could prove troublesome. Also stay away
from skis which have exposed screws, bolts or other hardware that
could possibly cause injury.

A pair of durable skis suitable for the beginner, complete with
bindings, should cost $40 to $50. Some manufacturers offer equipment
packages. Northland's "starter set" includes skis, a 75-foot towline,
the harness to attach it to the boat and a three-step boat ladder.

The towline should be about 75 feet long if you are using an
inboard boat, 60 feet long if it's an outboard. This assures that the
beginner will be skiing in smooth water between the wakes. These
lengths should also be used when an instructor is skiing with a pupil.

Polypropylene line is more popular than manila. It floats and, since
it comes in colors, is easily spotted in the water. Yellow is easier to
see than any other color.

THE TOW BOAT

The tow boat has to have sufficient power to be able to pull two
skiers—the pupil and his instructor—at a sustained speed of 25 mph.
Later, when the youngster is skilled enough to ski by himself, a speed
of up to 20 mph is all that is required.

The tow boat can be an inboard or outboard craft, but it should
have a steering wheel, which permits safer, more responsive steering
than a tiller. A boat with a wide transom will provide greater stability
and reduce the size of the wake. Low freeboard makes the boat easier
to climb in and out of. A rearview mirror, which permits the boat operator to observe the skier at all times, is a vital piece of equipment. The
mirror, however, shouldn't serve as a substitute for a second person
in the boat, an observer.

The hitch—the method of attaching the towline to the boat—must
be such that the pull is distributed evenly; otherwise the skier can cause

Water Skiing

the boat to capsize by pulling too much to one side. The simplest way of making the hitch is by means of an eyebolt mounted to the transom midway between the two sides and so positioned that the rope end is fixed about 3 inches above the transom. A harness between them is equipped with a free-riding swivel, and to this the towline is attached.

A third method, and one that is widely used, involves the use of metal rings fixed to each side of the motor well. Whatever type of hitch is used, be sure to check to see that there is no possibility that the line can become fouled in the propeller.

THE AMERICAN WATER SKI ASSOCIATION

If your youngster becomes serious about water skiing, it's a good idea to enroll him as a member of the American Water Ski Association (7th St. and Avenue G. Southwest, Winter Haven, Fla. 33880). Write for an application form. With membership, the youngster receives a year's subscription to *The Water Skier* (seven issues), several illustrated booklets covering different facets of skiing, an introduction to the AWSA rating system, and the right to enter AWSA-sanctioned tournaments. Individual membership costs $10. Family membership, which entitles a husband, wife and all children to membership privileges, is $20.

SKIING COMPETITION

The first national water-skiing tournament was held in 1939 at Jones Beach State Park, Long Island, New York, and except for the years of World War II, tournaments have been held annually ever since. The American Water Ski Association supervises tournament competition. There is a division for boys and girls age sixteen and under. Events include the slalom, a precision run between anchored buoys on a measured course; jumping for distance, in which contestants ascend a wooden jumping ramp; and trick riding, which involves stunts like holding the towline with one's foot, skiing backward, and executing a full turnaround off the jumping ramp.

BOOKS AND PUBLICATIONS

Surely the most comprehensive book on this activity is *The Complete Beginner's Guide to Water Skiing* (Doubleday, $7.95), by Al Tyll, four-time national men's track champion and holder of many regional skiing titles. The book contains more than 350 photographs and diagrams.

117

Let's Go Water Skiing (Hawthorn Books, $4.95), by Tom Hardman and Bill Clifford, contains detailed instruction and advice as well as background information on the sport. The American Water Ski Association offers thirty different booklets on various water-skiing topics. Among the free ones are "Water Skiing Fundamentals," "Safety in Water Skiing," and "Safe Boat Driving for Skiing."

IV SHOOTING SPORTS

RIFLERY
SHOTGUNNING

RIFLERY

Riflery, says Jim Dee, a well-known expert on marksmanship and recreational shooting, is "a clean, invigorating sport well suited to nearly everyone regardless of age, sex or physical capabilities."

Indeed, it is true. And riflery is more. It is a relaxing recreation, yet it probably teaches precision and attention to detail as well as a course in mathematical logic. Though riflery could never be classed as a strenuous sport, when combined with hunting it provides a fair amount of vigorous exercise. And whether one happens to be shooting in the field, forest or a neighborhood range, the sport helps improve the coordination of eye, mind, and muscle.

Riflery demands no particular amount of strength or stamina on the part of the participant, and one's sex is no barrier.

What the sport does require is a sense of responsibility. Would you leave your youngster in the house alone for two or three hours? Would you send him to the supermarket alone with a shopping list and a $10 bill? If the answer is yes, says the National Rifle Association, the youngster is ready for riflery, under proper supervision, of course.

Smallbore riflery could never be classed as an expensive activity. A .22 rifle costs less than a pair of junior skis; a round of ammunition, about 2¢.

121

There are plenty of facilities, probably many more than you realize. There are about 4200 junior range-firing programs operating, in which youngsters are instructed and supervised by adults. And these represent only the tip of the iceberg. The National Education Association supports a nationwide program to make outdoor education a part of the school curriculum, and the program puts the stress on shooting sports. More than 1500 summer camps offer instruction in riflery, and most camps boast their own ranges. Civic and service groups, veterans' organizations, police departments, fire departments and conservation organizations are among those that sponsor shooting programs.

It is not likely that you will be involved with rifles and shooting for very long without being exposed to the work of the National Rifle Association, an organization that is deeply interested in the safety and educational aspects of firearms use. You can call upon the organization to help you in many ways.

A nonprofit organization supported by the membership fees of individuals and clubs, the NRA is the industry-accepted source of information on shooting-club organization and operation, range instruction and procedure, and basic marksmanship training. *The American Rifleman,* a monthly magazine devoted exclusively to guns and shooting, is the official journal of the NRA. It is the recognized authority on guns, ammunition and shooting equipment, as on the techniques of field and target shooting.

Senior members of the NRA receive the publication without additional charge. Special reduced subscription rates are offered to junior members. Boys and girls who have not yet reached their eighteenth birthday are eligible for junior membership in the NRA. Full information on membership and on the organization and affiliation of junior and senior shooting or hunting clubs can be obtained by writing the organization. Its address is: 1600 Rhode Island Ave. N.W., Washington, D.C. 20036.

BUYING A RIFLE

Opinion is just about unanimous that the best rifle for beginners is the .22-caliber. It's precise and accurate, and thanks to its limited recoil and limited noise, it can be handled by a boy or girl of nine or ten.

And the .22 is almost maintenance-free. After a day on the range or in the field, all you have to do is put the gun back on the rack. Thanks to noncorrosive priming and rust-inhibiting lubricants, only an occasional cleaning is necessary.

Riflery

Give consideration to the youngster's size and strength when you're choosing a rifle. You want a rifle with some heft to it—indeed, a youngster should use the heaviest rifle that is comfortable for him—but it should not be so heavy that it is at all cumbersome, and useful only when firing from a prone position.

Be sure to take the youngster with you when you go to purchase the rifle. The butt of the stock should fit snugly to the child's shoulder. Don't let the salesman tell you that the child is supposed to adjust the manner in which he holds the rifle in order to get a comfortable fit.

While there are approximately seventy-five different .22 models in production, only about fifteen or twenty of these can be considered junior rifles. The NRA will send you a list of light .22 rifles, most of which are suitable for young shooters.

Remington offers a "Boy's Carbine," its model 514; Stevens has its "Youth Model," its 73Y. These are single-shot rifles capable of handling Short, Long or Long Rifle cartridges. They are priced at around $25.

Winchester's bolt-action Model 320, well suited for the pre-teener, weighs 5½ pounds. While the five-round magazine permits clip loading, it also single-loads easily. It can thus serve as both a training rifle and, once the basics have been learned, a repeater.

Some parents end up purchasing a standard-size .22 and then cutting down the stock to fit the young shooter, or they cut down one of their own rifles. To determine how much of the stock should be cut off, have the youngster hold the rifle by the pistol grip with his trigger hand and place the butt end at his hip. Using a felt-tip pen, mark the stock on a line just behind the bend of the child's elbow. This is where the stock should be cut. Use a hacksaw with a fine-tooth blade. Before sawing, wrap masking tape around the stock so that the cutting area is completely covered, which will prevent the wood from splintering as you saw. The final step is to remove and reattach the butt plate. Keep the sawed-off piece; you may want to reattach a portion of it when the child gets bigger.

It may also be necessary to build up the pistol-grip portion of the stock. This may even hold true in the case of a factory-built junior or youth rifle, for almost always these are simply adult rifles with shortened stocks. It is almost impossible for a very young shooter to get a comfortable grasp on the pistol grip while putting his index finger on the trigger. Use plastic wood to extend the grip forward. After the built-up area is sanded smooth, the stock itself should be stripped and refinished.

123

Of course, the length of the stock is only one topic you have to consider. Another is the rifle's action.

Look for a single-shot rifle with a bolt action. After a rifle of this type has been fired, you know for sure that all it contains is a spent cartridge. Another reason the single-shot style is good is that it gives importance to each shot. The user is much more likely to make each one count. A semi-automatic rifle, on the other hand, tends to encourage carelessness. Later on, once the youngster knows the basics, there is no harm in buying him a magazine- or clip-fed bolt-action or semi-automatic .22.

Types of rifles to avoid for the very young shooter are any of those that feature a slide action. With rifles of this type, the shooter pulls the handgrip on the barrel toward him to eject the empty cartridge, then pushes it forward to load a fresh cartridge into the chamber. The problem is that it is possible to have a cartridge in the magazine without realizing it, and this can be a real hazard in the case of a young shooter. Lever-action rifles have the same disadvantage.

While most experts advise that the novice shooter be provided with a bolt-action rifle, there sometimes are reasons for choosing a semi-automatic. The latter should be considered if your future plans include hunting expeditions for small game animals. With the semi-automatic, the shot and the sound of the action are all one noise, and the shooter can stay quietly concealed behind a log or bush should he miss with the first shot. But with a bolt-action, slide-action, or lever-action rifle, when the action closes on the new round there will be a second noise, and the game will flee.

You also have to decide on the matter of sights. Open sights are the most common. They usually consist of a metal bead or post front sight which is used in combination with a V-notched or U-notched rear sight. Next in popularity is the peep sight. In this combination, the front sight is the same as in open sights, but the rear sight consists of a tiny peephole through which the shooter looks.

The peep sight is best, whether your youngster is planning on target shooting in the future or hunting. The front sight can be either a short metal post or an aperture. The rear sight is the peep. It will probably take the form of a small hole in a metal disc. It should be sophisticated enough so that it can be adjusted for both elevation and windage, with reading in half-minutes of angle.

A third type of sight is the telescopic sight. What it does is enlarge the target. There's no aligning of the front and rear sights; all the shooter has to do is set the telescope crosshairs on the target.

Riflery

There can be no doubt that a youngster using a rifle equipped with a telescopic sight will enjoy quick success as a marksman, but there's a drawback. With the so-called iron sights—open sights or peep sights—a youngster is taught the importance of the proper grip and trigger squeeze. Another shortcoming of the telescope is that it's not as versatile in the field. So start your young shooter with an open sight or peep sight. Later he can switch to a scope. But going the other way, from a telescopic sight to an iron sight, isn't so simple.

AMMUNITION FOR THE .22

When it comes to .22 ammunition, there are three basic types— Shorts, Longs, and Long Rifles (LRs). The cartridge case for the Long is the same as that for the LR, but it shoots the same 29-grain bullet as the Short. The LR has a 40-grain bullet.

The Long's bullet has a muzzle velocity of 1240 feet per second (fps), 85 fps faster than the Short's bullet and 95 fps slower than the LR's bullet. Most rifles are more accurate with LRs than with either of the other two types.

Ammunition for the .22 is not expensive. The .22 Short usually costs about 92¢ a box (with 50 shells to a box). The Long lists at $1.01 a box, and the Long Rifle at $1.07. One way to keep down the cost of ammunition is to watch for sales at sporting goods stores or gun shops. One recent "special" featured LRs at $7 a carton (500 shells).

Some people say that the constant use of Shorts on a rifle chambered for LRs will cause corrosion in the forward part of the chamber. When LRs are again fired, they may stick. But experts declare that thanks to universal use of noncorrosive ammunition this isn't too likely any more.

GAS, PNEUMATIC AND AIR RIFLES

Some parents introduce their youngsters to shooting by means of a spring-operated rifle (the so-called BB gun) or a CO_2 or pneumatic rifle. These have a much lower velocity—300 to 600 fps—than the .22 and so much less distance is advisable between the firing line and target. This, plus the fact that these rifles make no explosive sound, makes them more adaptable for use in the basement or any large room.

The BB gun is well known. It is operated by compressing a spring (by means of the rifle's pump or lever action) that has a plunger head fixed to one end. Pulling the trigger releases the spring, which drives a column of air in front of it, propelling the shot through the smoothbore shot tube at about 300 fps.

Gas guns and airguns are much more advanced and must be handled with the same precautions as the rimfire .22 and other firearms. Gas guns are powered by CO_2 stored in a replaceable metal cartridge about the size of a shotgun shell. Airguns, or pneumatic guns, have a "pump-up" mechanism, which compresses air that is used to drive the load. Both types fire skirted lead pellets through a rifled barrel at velocities up to 600 fps. Obviously, neither is a toy.

The NRA has developed competitive shooting programs for guns of this type, one program on a 15-foot range, the other at 25 feet. Precision air rifles are used in the NRA's 10-meter competition. Targets for these programs bear scoring rings which are proportional in size to those on the standard .22-caliber 50-foot targets.

Airguns for beginners are priced at $25. A high-quality target airgun sells for about $90, and the most sophisticated models cost about twice that amount.

WHERE TO SHOOT

No one knows for sure just how many rifle and pistol ranges there are in the United States, but the number is well up in the thousands. There is sure to be a range close to you, whether you live in an urban, a suburban or rural area.

If you're not aware of one, simply look in your Yellow Pages under "Rifle and Pistol Ranges." Or you can write to the National Rifle Association and ask for information about rifle clubs in your area. Clubs have access to ranges.

Smallbore rifle ranges are of several different types. There are indoor gallery ranges at 50 and 75 feet, and outdoor ranges at 50 feet, 50 and 100 yards, and 50 meters. Finally, there are long ranges at 200 yards. Since the standard for junior shooting is 50 feet, youngsters can be accommodated at just about every range.

You can add to the enjoyment a youngster gets out of riflery by enrolling him in an NRA Junior Rifle Club. By bringing him in contact with other shooters of his age and experience, club membership will help to broaden his interest and increase his understanding of the sport.

There are more than 3000 chartered clubs in operation, and they vary widely in character. The minimum requisite is that the junior club be made up of "at least ten American citizens under the age of nineteen," supervised by an adult instructor. With virtually all clubs, the activities include instruction in the safe handling of firearms and in

accurate shooting. Often members fire for certification ratings of national significance, and participate in team and individual competitions. Fees and dues are fixed by the club, not by the NRA.

MARKSMANSHIP

Be sure that your youngster is taught to shoot by a certified instructor, or at least by an experienced marksman. It's disastrous to learn bad habits at the beginning. Novices want to jerk the trigger, not squeeze it, and unless the instructor realizes this and works to curb the tendency, your youngster will never be able to excel, even if he has perfect eyesight and perfect coordination.

127

Trigger squeeze is one of the three fundamentals of rifle shooting. The other two are aiming and holding. On every shot, the idea is to aim the rifle accurately, hold it steady, and then squeeze the trigger—so as not to upset either the aim or the hold. If the young shooter can learn these essentials, and learn to coordinate one with the other, he can become a good shot. This presupposes, of course, that he is thoroughly familiar with the mechanical aspects of the rifle, that the sights are properly adjusted, and, should he be shooting outdoors, that he knows how to adjust for windage.

The biggest problem that beginners have is holding the rifle steady. How do you solve this problem? By teaching the youngster to shoot from a prone position with a gunsling. "In this position," says Jim Dee, "not being bothered by holding difficulties, the beginner is able to apply himself to accurate aiming, to proper control of the trigger, and to their coordination.

"Then having learned how to make a small group of shots anywhere on the target, he can teach himself sight adjustment and learn to move the group promptly into the center of the bull's-eye."

It takes, according to Mr. Dee, about five days' practice, half an hour a day, for the novice to learn how to hold the rifle steady in the prone position. Real excellence, of course, takes experience.

COMPETITIVE SHOOTING

When the national rifle championships were held at Creedmore, New York, in 1872, they attracted more than 100,000 spectators. The winning marksmen were hailed as being "magnificent types of Americans" and were lionized at least as much as Babe Ruth and Jack Dempsey were to be in the 1920s.

While spectator interest in shooting competition may have dimmed somewhat, competition is much more widespread today than ever before. Thanks to the National Rifle Association and its system of approving and registering local tournaments, it is almost certain that you can find smallbore rifle competition for yourself and your youngster within easy driving range of your home just about any weekend of the year.

Although these tournaments may seem informal, they are conducted under NRA rules and supervised by NRA referees and other NRA-approved officials. Scores are reported to NRA headquarters and classified under a uniform grading system.

Junior competition. Competition for beginners is at a range of 50 feet using the official NRA "2-to-10" target in which the lowest

Riflery

value is 2, and the highest, the bull's-eye, is 10. More advanced juniors often use the 5-bull or 11-bull targets. The former bears five bull's-eyes, each the same size as those on the 2-to-10 target. The difference is that the outside rings, those having values of from 2 to 4 points, do not appear. The 11-bull target contains eleven bull's-eyes of this type.

These targets are used by NRA as the basis of its junior awards program, in which young shooters seek to qualify for each one of a series of marksmanship medals, pins, bars and brassards. Any .22-caliber rifle with a trigger pull of not less than three pounds and taking any .22-caliber factory-loaded rimfire ammunition can be used. The use of telescopic sights is not permitted.

Ten qualifying targets are required for each stage, with shooters using the position designated by the NRA for each. Here is a listing of the qualifying scores for each stage (the expression "20 x 50" means a score of 20 points out of a possible 50 points):

Stage	Position	Score
Pro-Marksman	Any	20 × 50
Marksman	Any	25 × 50
Marksman First Class	Any	30 × 50
Sharpshooter	Any	35 × 50
Bar I	Prone	40 × 50
Bar II	Sitting	30 × 50
Bar III	Sitting	35 × 50
Bar IV	Sitting	40 × 50
Bar V	Kneeling	30 × 50
Bar VI	Kneeling	35 × 50
Bar VII	Kneeling	40 × 50
Bar VIII	Standing	30 × 50
Bar IX	Standing	40 × 50
Distinguished Rifleman:		
	Prone	18 × 20 (per bull)
	Sitting	18 × 20 (per bull)
	Kneeling	16 × 20 (per bull)
	Standing	16 × 20 (per bull)

Targets must be fired at one at a time. If more than five shots appear on one bull's-eye, only the five lowest scores are counted. Shots which break or touch a line or circle are scored at the higher value.

Once the members of a club begin qualifying for individual awards, the club is ready to participate in national tournaments. The shooters fire at their home range and then the registered targets are mailed to NRA headquarters for scoring and ranking. Awards are sent to the winning teams.

When there are several junior clubs in the same area, teams of shooters often form a league and take part in regularly scheduled competition. League champions can compete against champions of other leagues.

ADDITIONAL INFORMATION

The NRA (address above) is your best source of information on firearms safety and use. The organization has available a remarkable assortment of literature. Write for a list of instruction materials. Three booklets are of particular interest: *Hunter Safety Handbook* (10¢), *Basic Rifle Marksmanship* (25¢), and *NRA Air Gun Program* (no charge).

An array of material is also available from the National Shooting Sports Foundation, Inc. (1075 Post Rd., Riverside, Conn. 06878). Write and request a catalog of publications.

The Sporting Arms and Ammunition Manufacturers' Institute (420 Lexington Ave., New York, N.Y. 10017) is a third organization that makes available booklets and brochures. Its *Handbook of Small Bore Rifle Shooting* is particularly good. Write for a publication catalog.

There is a great sense of accomplishment in shooting, even for the beginner. His satisfaction comes from putting a hole in a piece of paper at a precise point and knowing that it was, completely, a personal accomplishment. For those who wonder at being challenged by the necessity for putting a hole in a piece of paper at a particular spot, this exercise is one which attracts millions of people annually. It manifests itself in some people by making them try to put a golf ball in a hole. Others try to roll a bowling ball into a group of pins at a certain place.

—Stanley A. Mate
Director, Activities Division
National Rifle Association of America

SHOTGUNNING

The basic idea behind the shotgun is to enable the gunner to hit a moving target. It can be a rabbit bounding for a stone wall or a pheasant taking wing. But it doesn't necessarily have to be live. It can be a clay target, the type used in trap or skeet shooting.

A youngster can be taught to use a shotgun at eleven or twelve, or earlier if he's big enough to hold one. A more reliable rule of thumb says that when a child attains a weight of 80 pounds he should be able to handle a small-gauge shotgun and cope with the recoil without discomfort. It's important, of course, that the gun fit snugly to the youngster's shoulder; otherwise recoil will be a problem no matter the child's size. What's said here presupposes that the young shooter has sufficient emotional maturity to observe the rules of safe shooting and good sportsmanship.

The best type of shotgun for a youngster is the single-barreled, single-shot, break-open gun, a type readily available in junior sizes. Autoloading guns and pump guns are more popular, but for reasons of safety the single-shot type is recommended.

Gauge is the next thing to consider. The gauge number of a gun originally was determined by the number of round lead balls of a size just large enough to fit the bore of the gun, that constituted a pound.

131

For example, if it took twelve bore-size balls to weigh a pound, the gun would be 12-gauge. Nowadays, however, the gauge number denotes a precise barrel diameter; a 12-gauge barrel has an inside bore diameter of .729 inch. Modern gauges, beginning with the smallest, are 28, 20, 16, 12 and 10.

The one exception to the gauge designation is the .410, the smallest of the modern shotguns. The designation .410 is actually a caliber, since it means the bore diameter, .410 inches.

Unless your youngster is fairly big—100 pounds or more—stay away from the 12-gauge shotgun. The recoil is too great. But don't go too far in the other direction. Many well-meaning parents equip their youngsters with the .410. It's so light in weight that the smallest child can handle it with ease and the recoil is hardly noticeable, but the problem is that it throws such a small amount of shot that the youngster has to be a precision shooter in order to be able to hit anything. It's really not a beginner's gun; it's an expert's gun. This is especially true if you're planning clay-target shooting. The 28-gauge is also too small; though its diameter is considerably larger than the .410, its shells usually contain the same amount of shot.

It's better to choose a 20-gauge shotgun for the young beginner. The recoil from either isn't sufficient to cause him any great distress, and there are enough pellets in a load to give him an even chance.

Of course, the type of shooting that the child is going to be doing will help you in making your purchase. For instance, the 20-gauge gun is well suited for quail or grouse, but lacks the hitting power for waterfowl.

As far as trap shooting is concerned, small-gauge shotguns can be used for informal target games and competition, but in official events conducted under the rules of the Amateur Trapshooting Association only 12-gauge guns can be used. It's different with skeet; the National Skeet Shooting Association holds competition for 12-, 20- and 28-gauge guns and the .410.

You also have to make a decision as to the shotgun's choke. In the last several inches of its length, the inside diameter.of a choked gun barrel becomes smaller. The idea of choke is to constrict the shot pattern, to keep it closer together. Shotguns that produce the densest shot pattern have what is called full-choke barrels; next in order are improved-modified choke, modified choke, improved-cylinder choke (also called skeet #1), and cylinder (skeet #2). The cylinder bore has no choke at all.

Shotgunning

Here again the kind of shooting the child will be doing will guide you. If he is going to be pass-shooting at waterfowl, he undoubtedly will be shooting large birds at long range, and thus will require a full-choke barrel. But this type isn't recommended for quail or grouse; the pattern is so dense that it will mutilate the game, and it is easier to hit the target with a broader pattern.

The type of shooting also determines the kind of ammunition to buy—that is, the pellet size. For example, No. 6 shot is usually prescribed for hunting rabbits and squirrels; No. 7½, which is smaller, is for trap shooting.

SHOTGUN SAFETY

Once the matter of equipment is settled, the next step is to expose the young shooter to the National Rifle Association's Hunter Safety Course, which is meant to teach safe hunting procedures and a responsible attitude toward the sport. While the course doesn't attempt to make each participant an expert marksman, some "how to shoot" information is given. The course lasts several hours. Inquire at your local gun shop or rifle range as to whether there is a certified course instructor in your area. Write the National Rifle Association (1600 Rhode Island Ave. N.W., Washington, D.C. 20036) and request a copy of the Hunter Safety Handbook (it costs 10¢). It will give you detailed information on what the course contains.

Statistics indicate that more than half of all firearms accidents occur in the home. Aware of this, the NRA has developed its Home Firearm Safety Course. It covers such topics as the storage of guns and ammunition and the safety aspects of gun cleaning. It also includes a demonstration of the different types of gun actions, and a session in which the participants, using dummy ammunition, load and unload various kinds of firearms. No active shooting is done in the course, and as a result it can be presented in one's home, at a school, or at a community center.

If your youngster is twelve to eighteen years old, ask at your local gunshop or sporting goods store whether a Teen Hunters Club is being planned for your locality. The Shooting Development Department of Winchester-Western helps get clubs organized and maintains an active interest in their success. Local civic or service groups often act as co-sponsors.

The club's activities occupy one full day in which groups of a hundred or so boys and girls are instructed in some of the basics of

133

gun handling, hunting safety and shooting fun. There are lectures, demonstrations and live shooting at clay and paper targets. NRA instructors who participate often make arrangements for continuing safety or competitive shooting programs. For more information, including advice on how to organize a Teen Hunters Club, write Winchester's Shooting Development Department (275 Winchester Ave., New Haven, Conn. 06504).

You should also find out whether a Winchester Father and Son Shooting and Hunting Seminar is being planned for your area. In this program, father-youngster pairs are brought together at a local gun club for a day or weekend of concentrated instruction in gun handling and safety. The program also includes live shooting at clay targets. Write to Winchester for additional information.

Even though you yourself may be experienced in the handling of guns, and your son has been thoroughly trained in the safety aspects of shooting, you always have to be on guard. If your child wants to bring one of his companions into the field, be sure he is responsible and knows how to handle a gun safely.

SOME FUNDAMENTALS

The basic idea in shooting with a shotgun is to put the shot charge where the target is going to be rather than where it is at the instant the trigger is pulled. This can be a difficult concept for the beginner to grasp. Evidence of this is the fact that most novices miss because they shoot behind the target, way behind.

Pointing and firing a shotgun puts the user in the same situation as a quarterback who is throwing to a receiver breaking across the field. He has to throw to the point where the receiver is going to be, not to the receiver himself. Or it's like a person with a hose who tries to spray a stream of water at another. The target is not apt to be stationary, so he has to be able to lead the target with the stream.

Instructors in the use of the shotgun recognize three different methods of solving this problem, three shooting techniques. There is spot shooting, in which the shooter, at the instant he sees the target, snaps the gun to his shoulder, anticipates where the shot charge and target will meet, and fires. It's done almost instinctively. Only experienced shooters can expect to be successful with this method.

A second method is called pointing out. In this, the shooter determines the angle of his target, its speed and its range, and while he is doing so he starts to swing his gun. He swings it past the target,

Shotgunning

and then shoots ahead of it. This method, too, is for the more experienced gunner.

For beginners, the third technique, known as the swing-through method, is recommended. The shooter sights his target and swings the barrel along its path of flight, catching up with it and passing it. As the barrel goes by the target, he pulls the trigger, then keeps the barrel moving in a follow-through motion. Reduced to its essentials, the method is as follows:

1. Sight the target.
2. Swing the barrel with the target.
3. Swing the barrel past the target and fire.
4. Keep swinging.

In teaching this method, be sure that your youngster keeps his head on the stock. If he lifts his head, his eyes will stay on the target but the gun barrel won't.

Real success comes with consistency, using the same stance, the same amount of lead, and the same style of shooting on every pull of the trigger. And consistency comes with practice.

SHOTGUN HUNTING

It would take a book at least twice the size of this one to set down the individual hunting conditions and regulations for each of the fifty states. Alaska is endowed with an enormous variety of game; only recently did Rhode Island begin to offer a limited deer season. Nebraska welcomes nonresident hunters; Minnesota discourages them. Some states have burgeoning game populations, whitetail deer, in particular; other states face critical shortages, especially in the case of upland birds.

What you have to do is write to the Fish and Game Department of the state in which you plan to hunt, and ask for a copy of the regulations covering fees, licenses, seasons and gun use.

One significant development must be mentioned. As hunting land has become scarcer, more and more hunters are pursuing the sport on hunting preserves. A preserve consists of a large tract of land that is operated by an individual or group under a state license. Only Alaska, Maine, Idaho and North Dakota are without laws providing for the operation of such preserves.

The preserve operator raises or buys game birds, which he releases according to the number of hunters he expects. Pheasants are

the principal birds provided on preserves, and chukar partridge and quail are not uncommon. Some preserves offer ducks, turkey and even deer.

The fees vary but usually range from $4 to $7 per bird released. The seasons vary, too, but from September to April is usual.

The National Shooting Sports Foundation, Inc. (1075 Post Rd., Riverside, Conn. 06878) will provide you with a free directory of the country's shooting preserves. An updated edition is published in September each year.

TRAP AND SKEET

At its modern headquarters complex in Vandalia, Ohio, the Amateur Trapshooting Association boasts a Hall of Fame where the visitor can see displayed some of the original glass balls that traps once threw, the later clay balls, and the first clay discs. Perhaps some of the most fascinating items are the oil portraits of the sport's past champions and

Shotgunning

old programs from the first tournaments. Trapshooting is about two hundred years old and it has a rich history.

Throughout most of the present century, women have played an important role. In 1915, one Plinky Topperwein shot at 8,010 birds and broke 95 percent of them. It is said that even Annie Oakley held Mrs. Topperwein in awe.

Skeet is of a more recent vintage, dating from the early 1900s. The same clay birds are used as in trap, and they are thrown in the same way, using the same type of powerful spring catapult. The chief difference is that the shooter does his firing from each one of eight different stations on a semicircular course. The National Skeet Shooting Association was formed in 1927.

The clay-target sports are more popular today than ever before, and one reason is that they provide family members with an opportunity to compete on about an equal basis. Boys and girls often do as well or better than their parents. There has been a number of instances in recent years where major trap and skeet events have been won by teen-agers.

Strength and stamina aren't necessary to be successful in the clay-target sports. Even a physically handicapped youngster can do well. A child can begin as soon as he is big enough to hold a shotgun. Emotional maturity is a vital factor, not only as regards the safety aspects of the sport; the shooter has to be able to concentrate intently and at will. If he is unable to focus his attention on each target as it's thrown, then instruction is a lost cause.

If you put your youngster in the hands of a good instructor, he will begin breaking targets right away. The challenge of improving never really diminishes. Aside from the excitement that trap and skeet provide in themselves, each of these sports can be valuable in making a youngster proficient with a shotgun, in prepping him for hunting. Of course, many people who shoot clay targets never pursue live game.

Essentially, all you need for clay-target shooting is a shotgun, shells, a carton of targets, a hand trap, and a few acres of flat terrain with a safety zone of about 300 yards. Facilities of this type are available at trap and skeet ranges, most of which are to be found within convenient driving distances of major cities. (They're listed in the Yellow Pages under "Trap and Skeet Ranges.") Depending on where you live, most are open on weekends all year. Some are equipped with lights for night shooting.

What type of clay target shooting is best for the beginner—trap or skeet? If you're like most parents you'll teach your youngster the

137

one that you know best. But your overall objective should be to help him learn how to hit moving targets with some degree of consistency as quickly as possible; otherwise, discouragement can set in.

With this in mind, consider that standard trapshooting is done from the 16-yard line using a 12-gauge, full-choked shotgun. Since the majority of youngsters can't handle the recoil of the 12-gauge gun, they have to be equipped with something less, and this makes the targets difficult to bring down.

But in skeet, the targets are shot at from each one of eight different range stations, and the youngster gets a much better chance. For one thing, small-gauge guns are permitted in skeet, so the young shooter isn't going to be penalized. More important, you can move the youngster around from one station to the next, beginning with the simplest and moving to the more difficult ones in stages. For example, Station 7 is considered to be the easiest on the standard round. Targets are launched straight away from the shooter; he doesn't have to be concerned about lead. Even shooters who have had no experience in skeet shooting can bring down targets out of Station 7. Let your youngster

Shotgunning

master Station 7 before moving on to the next more difficult location, Station 1.

What you should avoid is having the youngster work with an instructor who takes him through the course in the standard sequence right from the start. He'll break a few, but very few.

Both skeet and trap offer organized competition for youngsters. These are the age groups that are frequently used:

	Skeet	Trap
Sub-junior	under 13	under 15
Junior	under 17	15 to 18

Trap and skeet each have their own governing organizations, and both will provide you information of a general nature. For trap, it's the Amateur Trapshooting Association (P.O. Box 246, Vandalia, Ohio 45377). The organization formulates the rules for the sport, gives advice on range-building, supervises and sanctions shoots held by local and state organizations, and annually sponsors the Grand American Trapshooting Tournament. Held in Vandalia, Ohio, it attracts more than 4,500 participants each year who fire more than 2,000,000 shotgun shells during the nine-day tournament period. The ATA publishes a monthly magazine, *Trap and Field,* and also *Official Trapshooting Rules,* an annual.

The National Skeet Shooting Association (2608 Inwood Road, Dallas, Texas 75235) enforces the rules of skeet shooting and supervises and sanctions tournament competition.

139

V OUTDOOR ACTIVITIES

BOATING
SAILING
CANOEING
BACKPACKING
FISHING
BICYCLING

BOATING

Boating has been booming for well over a decade now and shows no signs of slumping. In 1972, the pleasure-boat industry reported a 25 percent increase in sales over 1971. Some 46 million Americans have taken to the waterways in one form or another.

According to the National Association of Engine and Boat Manufacturers, the country's recreational fleet now numbers more than 9 million craft of all types. The total breaks down as follows: 5,420,000 outboard boats; 700,000 inboards, including documented yachts and auxiliary-power sailboats; 690,000 unpowered sailboats; and 2,400,-000 rowboats, canoes, dinghies and miscellaneous craft. I cite these statistics as evidence of boating's great diversity. The word "boat" can mean many things.

Boats for children can be simple or sophisticated. For a boy or girl of nine or ten, buy a folding boat or an inflatable. Older children, however, will look upon these as mere toys (which they are not); they'll want a fiberglass dinghy, a zippy sailboat, or maybe even a classy runabout with outboard power.

A folding boat consists of a fold-up wooden frame over which is stretched canvas or rubberized fabric. Most dealers offer two hull styles—a square-transom model that can be used with a small outboard or a double-ended kayak. The advantage of these craft is that they store and carry easily. The disadvantage is that they are fragile, and because they are so light in weight, they handle poorly in the wind.

Inflatables are better. Important technical advances have been made in this field in the last decade, and today's inflatables are sturdy, leakproof and virtually untippable and unsinkable. Rowing one is like paddling around in an inner tube. Some are equipped with motor mounts.

Boats of this type can be as simple as Gloy's Pioneer II, which is priced at $60, with paddles. It is 86 inches long and 46 inches wide, weighs 20 pounds, and features "duo-chamber" construction, which means it has a separate inflated inner core. Inflatable seats are fore and aft and there is a wooden foot rest in between.

Inflatables are easy to transport, of course. Just remember that they take time to set up and blow up.

BUYING A POWERED BOAT

For the teen-aged boy or girl who lacks the patience necessary to operate a sailboat or the muscle power to drive a canoe, or just happens to want a motor-driven craft, your best bet is an outboard-powered runabout. A rig of this type is not expensive. It can be purchased for from $300 up to $1,200, depending on the type of boat you want, wood or plastic, and the size of the engine.

For a beginner, a wooden boat 12 to 16 feet in length with a motor of 20 to 30 horsepower is what is recommended. In most cases, this means that the engine will have to be started manually (by a cord) and steered by a tiller. If the cost is not a major consideration, purchase a larger motor, one that starts at the press of a button and that can be rigged to steer from a seat up front. Cables link the steering wheel to the rudder. A built-in clutch with a three-position gearshift is another feature that is likely to be included.

Either type of outboard is simple to operate. The smaller engines have no reverse but they negotiate a tight 360-degree turn.

Wood is recommended over fiberglass because it is less expensive. Safety used to be a second factor; wood floats. But Coast Guard regulations, which became effective on July 1, 1973, specify that any powerboat under 20 feet in length that does not have positive flotation cannot be sold. So manufacturers now offer a wide array of unsinkable fiberglass boats. They still have not solved the problem of price, however.

Boating

Boats are also made of aluminum. Because they're light in weight, they are easy to trailer or load onto a cartop carrier. But their lightness makes aluminum boats difficult to handle in rough water. For saltwater use, they have to be treated with anticorrosive protection.

The hull bottom should be either V-shaped or rounded up forward, and flatten out from a point amidships sternward. With a hull bottom of this design, the forward portion of the craft lifts out of the water as power builds, and the hull skims efficiently over the surface. This is known as the planing effect.

In construction of a wooden hull, strips of wood, known as strakes, are sometimes laid one over another like clapboards on the side of a house. This is known as lapstrake construction and is the sturdiest, most durable type of wood construction. Lapstrake boats can handle waves and choppy water, and are recommended for boating on large lakes or ocean inlets.

In what is known as a carvel hull, the strakes are laid side by side, the edges are beveled, and the joints are calked and then sanded smooth. Boats of this type must be used in calmer waters. When you visit your local boat dealer, you may also see plywood hulls. Hulls of this type are lighter in weight than either of the other two and thus provide for higher performance. But there's the other side of the coin; because of their lightness, plywood craft don't handle well in strong winds or heavy weather of any type. They also have more of a tendency to leak or warp, which can mean repairs and the related expenses.

Check to see that the boat's transom—the notched-out wall at the stern on which the motor is mounted—is at least 20 inches high from top to bottom. This is especially important if rough water is expected. With anything less than 20 inches in height, you may be inviting an excess of water to wash over the stern. Check also for a self-draining well within the transom; all newer boats have one.

Any boat you buy for a beginner should have plenty of freeboard. When your youngster stands up in it, the gunwales should reach to a point above his knees, maybe even to thigh level. This will help to prevent him from falling out when attempting to land a fish. It also keeps spray from washing in. A spray rail, a strip of wood mounted on the hull exterior just above the waterline, will also help to keep the spray off the passengers and crew.

If your youngster is going to be using the boat only as a fishing rig, a motor of 10 to 12 horsepower should be sufficient. Light in weight and economical, it will send a 14-footer along at speeds of from 10 to 15 knots. If the boat is to be used for towing water skiers, more power is required, enough to give a sustained speed of 25 knots.

145

PERSONAL FLOTATION DEVICES

The Federal Boat Safety Act, which became effective in 1971, requires every recreational boat to carry at least one Coast Guard-approved flotation device for each person aboard. Three states—Texas, Utah and Nebraska—have passed laws requiring that children *wear* flotation devices when aboard boats.

Late in 1973, the Coast Guard updated regulations concerning flotation gear, reclassifying the different types and making recommendations as to which are acceptable for boats of various sizes. Life jackets, preservers, vests and other such equipment are now termed "personal flotation devices" (PFDs) by the Coast Guard, and each is labeled as to its type and performance.

The four types of PFDs that have been approved are:

Type I, Life Preservers. These are the big, bulky and sometimes uncomfortable orange-colored jackets that you see on ships. While they get low marks from a fashion standpoint, they give maximum buoyancy and maximum "positive righting movement," which means that one will turn you face-up in about five seconds if you happen to be unconscious. They're what you and the other members of your family should have if you expect to encounter hazardous boating conditions. The cost: $14 to $20.

Type II, Buoyant Vests. The vest is less—less buoyant, with less righting ability, and the cost is less, too, between $4 and $15. Vests are adequate for offshore use, fine for youngsters.

Type III, Special Purpose. These are for people whose boating is restricted to calm waters not many miles from the dock, and who find it uncomfortable or lacking in chic to wear Type I or Type II PFDs. Type III includes short-sleeved vests, long-sleeved coats (for winter sailing), and jump jackets (for water skiing). Ski belts, which are favored by some water skiers, are not approved by the Coast Guard. Type III PFDs are available in a variety of colors and sizes. They are easier to swim with but most models do not have the capability to turn you face-up if you're unconscious. The price can be another drawback. Type III vests cost from $18 to $30; coats, $45 to $55.

Type IV, Throwables. Rings, cushions, spherical or egg-shaped buoys, and horseshoes and anything else not meant to be worn but thrown to someone in the water belong in this category. Types I, II and III are made to "float the wearer indefinitely"; Type IVs aren't, and that is their great failing. They cost from $8 to $40.

Boating

Once you've decided on a type of wearable PFD that best suits your needs and those of the other members of your family, take the time to get a proper fit. Most life preservers and buoyant vests are labeled "adult" (for any person weighing over 90 pounds), "child" (for supporting 50 to 90 pounds) or "small child" (for youngsters less than 50 pounds). But consider these very general guidelines. Have your youngster try on any jacket or vest you plan to buy. Be sure that it fits snugly around the waist so that there is no chance the child will wind up with more flotation in back than in front.

Have your youngster practice donning his PFD. Have him practice in the dark. Have him try it out in shallow water.

BOATING INSTRUCTION

Courses in boating instruction are not difficult to find. Inquire at your local branch of the American Red Cross or find out whether there is a U.S. Coast Guard Auxiliary in your area.

147

The United States Power Squadrons, an organization of 83,000 boatmen dedicated to boating safety, offers free educational programs for men, women and youngsters age twelve or older. The course of instruction covers such topics as boat handling, seamanship, rules of the road, running lights, etc. After attending the twelve lectures that make up the course, a junior skipper receives an apprentice rating.

To find out whether a course is to be offered in your area, write the United States Power Squadrons (Box 345, Montvale, N.J. 07645) or simply place a toll-free call to the organization's information service. The number is: 800-243-6000.

Many state agencies offer boating instruction, too. For example, New York State's Division of Marine and Recreational Vehicles has a course for youngsters between ten and fourteen years of age. It stresses boating safety. Classes are conducted in every county of the state by volunteer instructors. In one recent year, 22,432 youngsters

earned their Young Boatman's Safety Certificates. More significantly, none of the first 100,000 youngsters to earn their certificates has been involved in a serious boating accident.

INSTRUCTION BOOKS, GUIDES AND DIRECTORIES

A visit to your local bookstore or neighborhood library will confirm the great number of books available on boating and related topics. You can get a complete rundown on what's available by obtaining a catalog published by the Boatman's Bookstore (21 West 46th St., New York, N.Y. 10036). Send 25¢ to cover handling and postage.

A less comprehensive but still helpful catalog is available from Motor Boating and Sailing Books (P. O. Box 2316, New York, N.Y. 10019). It's free.

These are among the recommended titles in the boating field:

Piloting, Seamanship and Small Boat Handling, (Hearst Books, $8.95) by Charles Chapman, has been, since 1922, the classic book in the field. Used as a textbook by both the U.S. Power Squadrons and the U.S. Coast Guard Auxiliary, it has grown to 700 pages, and rightly ranks as the most authoritative and comprehensive volume to be published on pleasure boats and boating. At $8.95, it's a terrific bargain.

Practical Boating; Inland and Offshore; Power and Sail (Doubleday, $7.95), by W. S. Kals, is an informative and often amusing volume by an experienced boatman that covers a variety of topics many other books neglect. It has especially helpful chapters on navigation and the handling of emergencies.

Primer of Navigation (Van Nostrand Reinhold, $13.50), by G. Mixer, is the pre-eminent volume on celestial navigation and piloting; it also discusses up-to-date techniques in radio, loran and radar navigation.

The Boat Owner's Maintenance Manual (De Graff, $12.50), by J. F. Toghill, covers the upkeep of engines, hulls, sails and spars.

If you're planning on buying a new boat, don't fail to obtain a copy of *Boat Owners Buyer's Guide,* an annual published by Yachting Publishing Corp. (50 West 44th St., New York, N.Y. 10036). It costs $1.50.

For information on navigation, navigational aids and rules of the road, obtain a copy of the *Recreational Boating Guide* (CG 340) from the Superintendent of Documents (U.S. Government Printing Office, Washington, D.C. 20025). Enclose 40¢.

SAILING

It's not difficult to understand why sailing is so popular with young people. Sailing is stimulating; it never fails to provide a challenge. Each puff of wind, each ripple of current, each wave is different. Every time a sailor takes his boat out he learns something new. The excitement never diminishes. A child can become wholly absorbed in the sport.

And sailing has real values, too. It demands skill and alertness, teaches self-reliance, and even helps to develop leadership qualities.

Sailing instruction is not difficult to find. National organizations such as the Boy Scouts of America, the National YMCAs and the Red Cross offer sailing instruction as part of their safety and education programs. Contact a local unit for information. In many areas of the country, adult-education courses are given at local high schools on weekends or in the evening. Some high schools now have sailing as part of their regular curriculum.

Also investigate whether there are commercial sailing schools in your area. These usually give thorough and practical instruction. Rates vary widely depending on the amount of instruction given and the type of equipment used. One school offers a comprehensive "Master's Course," four students to a class, which consists of five four-hour sessions, with about 85 percent of the time spent on the water. Tuition

Sailing

is $140. The Offshore Sailing School (5 East 40th St. New York, N.Y. 10016) and the New York Sailing School (340 Riverside Dr., New York, N.Y. 10025) are two popular commercial schools. Write for free catalogs.

It is not generally realized, but the United States Power Squadrons (Box 345, Montvale, N.J. 07645) offers instruction in sailboats and sailboating. The course, however, is one of the organization's electives, offered only to those who have completed the basic twelve-lecture boating course.

Whether or not your youngster is formally instructed, he or she should understand the aerodynamics of sailing before stepping into the boat for the first time. While a youngster usually has no trouble understanding how the wind powers the boat downwind, coming from behind the sail, it can be difficult to understand the movement that results when the wind blows across the sail. A force results from the pressure difference between the windward side of the sail (the side from which the wind is blowing) and the leeward side. This force, which is the same as the force that lifts an airplane's wing, is what enables a boat to sail into the wind.

The beginning sailor should be instructed in the physical principles of the centerboard, and how it works to reduce the sideways pressure of the wind. Tacking and heeling should be explained in depth before they're attempted.

BUYING A SAILBOAT

Take your time in selecting a boat for your youngster. Know the answers to these questions: Will more than one person be using the boat? How far does the child plan on cruising? Will he be using it for racing? A local boatyard or marine dealer will explain to you the types of sailboats best suited for the area's water and weather conditions.

For a teen-age boy or girl, consider a racing boat first. Racers are high-performance craft of proven merit.

Racers are divided into classes, which gives a boy or girl a certain kinship with other youngsters who own boats of the same type. Some of the more popular classes, with the approximate fleet size of each, are as follows: Snipe (15 feet 6 inches), 13,400; Comet (14 feet 6 inches), 4,000; Lightning (19 feet), 9,000; and Enterprise (13 feet 3 inches), 7,800. Prices range from $1,500 to $2,000.

Nearly all the smaller racers belong to one design class, which means that the official specifications for that class must be adhered

to in the construction of each boat. Boats of this type provide for exciting competition within individual classes, for the craft are all so similar that a race's outcome depends on sailing skill. Other racing boats belong to restricted classes. This means that there can be variations in certain aspects of construction and design. *The Sailboat Classes of North America* (Doubleday, $9.95), by Fessenden Blanchard, is a splendid book on the subject.

For younger beginners, a dinghy or a pram is recommended. These are smaller, lighter in weight, and easier to manage than the racers. Most are fiberglass and have single cat-rigged sails. They range in size from 7 to 14 feet and in price from $400 to $750. One of the most popular dinghies is the Penguin, which also happens to be a one-design boat. Just 11½ feet in length and weighing only 135

152

pounds, it can be sailed in comfort by a youngster and adult together. Penguins are available everywhere at about $650. Another appealing sailing dink is the Cape Dory 10, a fiberglass hull with a mahogany-trimmed interior that sells for $575.

Prams are usually flat or V-bottomed, wide-beamed, square at the stern, and have a blunted bow. One good feature is price. The Optimist, one of the best known of all prams, costs about $200.

Catamarans and sailboards, often called fun boats, are two reasons for the ever-increasing interest in sailing. A catamaran consists of two narrow hulls with a deck in between. They are fast but they lack the responsiveness of conventional sailboats. Prices range from $600 for a 12-footer up to approximately $2,000 for an 18-footer.

A sailboard is little more than a flat smooth-surfaced board fitted with a sail. They are fast, sporty and less expensive than most other types of sailboats. Kids love 'em. They usually range from 10 to 14 feet in length and are priced from $200 to $600. One disadvantage of sailboards is that they are wet and tippy. They thus must be considered warm-weather craft.

INSTRUCTION BOOKS

The Sailing Book Division of *Sail* magazine (38 Commercial Wharf, Boston, Mass. 02110) offers a wide selection of books on sailing. Write for a free catalog. These are among the recommended titles:

154

Sailing

Basic Sailing (Hearst Books, $2.50), by M. B. George, is a big, amply illustrated book that introduces the novice to the sailboat and proceeds to instruct him to a point where he can take the helm with confidence. Subjects covered include types of boats and sails; steering in fair weather and foul; raising and lowering sail; and handling multihull craft. It's on everyone's recommended list.

Invitation to Sailing (Simon and Schuster, $3.95), by Alan Brown, takes the form of a complete course in sailing instruction, from the fundamentals to racing tactics. A final section discusses the organization of a junior sailing program.

Another volume that can prove extremely helpful is *The Sailboat & Sailboat Equipment Directory,* an annual publication of *Sail* magazine. A copy of the current issue costs $2.

You can obtain a good deal of free and worthwhile background information on sailing from the American Sailing Council, which maintains its headquarters in the offices of the National Association of Engine and Boat Manufacturers (420 Lexington Ave., New York, N.Y. 10017). The Council will send you a list of sailboat builders and the types of boats each builds, a list of schools that offer sailing instruction, and several booklets covering other sailing topics.

CANOEING

The modern American canoe bears about as much similarity to the frail craft used by the Indians as the tepee does to a sprawling ranch-type house or split-level. Tippiness is a thing of the past. By increasing the beam of the canoe at a point just above the waterline, manufacturers have, in effect, endowed the canoe with a pontoonlike quality. When weight is shifted to one side or the other, the craft's expanded sides come in contact with the water's surface, imparting a stabilizing effect. Some canoes are so stable that a person can sit on a gunwale without tipping the craft over.

Some aluminum and fiberglass canoes have flotation tanks fore and aft. Even when full of water, they will support two passengers. Canoes of wood, of course, have flotation qualities that are about the same.

Despite the innovations in construction and design, modern canoes are sleek and graceful, and cut through the water with ease. Canoeing can be an enjoyable sport for any boy or girl who knows how to swim.

Besides being safe, modern canoes are wonderfully versatile. They provide efficient transportation over inland waters of all types, skimming the surface of mirrorlike lakes or negotiating tricky rapids. There

Canoeing

is nothing to equal the canoe when it comes to camping and back-country travel. Because they're so light, canoes are easy to carry atop an automobile for transport to one's favorite fishing grounds. Some can handle outboard motors. Others can be equipped with leeboards and sliding ballast and thus can be sailed.

When selecting a canoe for a youngster, you must take into consideration where the canoe is to be used (that is, the type of water that is to be encountered), the number of persons that are to be using the craft, and the general use to which it is going to be put. Once you know these things, you can make a judgment as to size, material, and type of canoe required.

A canoe meant for use on a small lake, by a teen-age boy or girl and a friend or two, doesn't have to be large; a 14-footer will do nicely. As for material, choose fiberglass. It's sturdy and doesn't need maintenance. In the case of a larger lake, one where good-size waves can kick up, a canoe with a broader beam is needed, at least a 17-footer and perhaps one that is as long as 19 feet.

For river use, it's aluminum. It's strong and it's light in weight. Should the craft collide with a rock, it will merely dent. Wood can split, fiberglass can fracture. Aluminum is also recommended because it makes portages easier. A pair of sixteen-year-olds can tote a 16-foot aluminum canoe without great difficulty.

Check the canoe's keel when making your purchase. A canoe designed for river use, no matter the material, will have what is known as a shoe keel. About 2 inches wide and only ¼ or ⅜ inch thick, it provides a certain amount of protection to the bottom and aids in directional movement, but it does not hinder the maneuverability required for river travel. The keel of a lake canoe is about twice as thick.

All of the major canoe manufacturers offer square-sterned models to accommodate motor mounts. Three horsepower is about all that is needed for a 14- or 16-foot craft. A 19-footer used by two or three passengers needs a 5-horse motor.

It must be said that square-sterned canoes don't paddle quite as easily as those of traditional design. They don't feel like a canoe; they're less responsive. They can even be troublesome if used on a downstream run in fast water, for water can back up against the flat stern surface, thus boosting the craft's speed and reducing control.

Have your youngster wear lightweight shoes when canoeing, light enough to swim in. Some sporting goods stores stock special canoe moccasins. While they are soft and flexible, they are so designed and

Canoeing

constructed that they give sufficient foot protection for short portages, even over rocky terrain. Crepe-soled canvas-top sneakers are an adequate substitute.

PADDLES

The best paddles are made of maple, but ash or close-grained spruce are acceptable. The blade should not be more than 6 inches in width, and its length should not be more than one-third of the paddle's length.

Check the grain. A straight grain makes for the strongest paddle. Cross-graining indicates weakness. Check also for signs of splitting.

The length of the paddle depends on the height of the person who is to use it. One rule of thumb states that the bow paddle should reach from the ground to the paddler's shoulders; the stern paddle should be longer, extending to the user's hairline. The extra length is needed in the stern to provide efficient steering.

PADDLE STROKES

If you teach your youngster the basic strokes, he will be able to handle the canoe in most situations. There are the forward strokes (for straight-ahead travel); the draw strokes (for turning); and jams (for stopping). There are variations, too, but these will come with practice.

The best way to begin is to have the youngster spend an hour or so sitting amidships watching experienced paddlers. Have him spend the first thirty minutes facing forward and watching the bow paddler, then have him turn around and face aft and observe the man in the stern. In this way he'll get an idea of the technique involved, the use of the upper body, and the angle and direction of the strokes.

The forward stroke, because it is used almost all of the time, is the most important of all. Sometimes it's referred to as the cruising stroke. When performed by the paddler in the bow, it involves grasping the paddle with one hand on the paddle's throat just above the blade, and the other hand on the paddle grip. The upper hand takes a firm grip, while the grip of the lower hand is looser, so as to permit the blade to be twisted to the right or left when necessary.

In executing the stroke, the upper hand should thrust the blade into the water, the paddler bending forward at the waist. The lower arm remains straight until the paddler begins the stroke, in which he pulls the blade as far as his hip. He then withdraws the blade and begins the next stroke.

A canoe paddle exerts force on only one side of the craft, so if the man in the bow is stroking on the right side the man in the stern must stroke from the left. But the stern man has a mechanical advantage—so much of an advantage that his stroke controls the direction of the boat. To compensate, he must perform a stroke that is somewhat different from the bow man's stroke. It begins in the same fashion, but as the blade reaches the paddler's hip he twists the handle so as to curl the blade away from the canoe. This overcomes the canoe's tendency to swing in the opposite direction.

A pre-teen-age child who masters this stroke—the J stroke, as it is often called—can handle a canoe on a pond or a calm lake. River travel requires more experience.

The draw stroke, used to change direction abruptly, is easy to learn. In this, the man in the bow positions the blade so that it is parallel to the canoe's centerline, thrusts the paddle into the water not forward of his body but straight out, in a direction away from the canoe, and then pulls the blade toward him. If the bow paddler is paddling on the right side, the bow will veer to the right. To hasten the turn, the man in the stern, paddling on the same side as the man in the bow, pushes away from the canoe, a stroke that is sometimes called a pry. A draw and a pry together can swing a canoe around within its own length.

The jam works to brake the canoe. The paddler simply positions the blade so that it is perpendicular to the centerline, and then thrusts it into the water at a point just forward of his hip. He then hooks the thumb of his lower hand over the gunwale, so as to aid the upper hand in preventing paddle movement. When both the bow and stern paddlers jam and hold, they can bring the craft to a stop within a distance shorter than the canoe's own length. Beginners often try to stop by backpaddling, but the jam is the more efficient method.

THE AMERICAN CANOE ASSOCIATION

To those interested in canoeing, either as a recreational activity or a competitive sport, the American Canoe Association (4260 East Evans Ave., Denver, Colo. 80222) offers a good many services and benefits. The organization invites individuals and groups to apply for membership. A junior membership is $2. Each member receives a one-year subscription to *American Canoeist,* the ACA's bimonthly magazine.

The organization sells and distributes instruction books and has available fifty or so monographs, with titles such as "Racing Paddling,"

Canoeing

"Cruising the Delaware" and "Canoe Cookery." Write for a free catalog. The ACA will also give you information about canoe clubs and the availability of canoe instruction in your area.

COMPETITION

Canoe competition—events such as the one-man single blade, two-man single blade, and the one- and two-man kayak—has a long history in many countries of Europe, but in the United States there have never been more than ten thousand or so competitors, a figure that includes weekend paddlers. However, the fact that the International Olympic Committee selected white-water canoeing as a competitive event in the 1972 Games did trigger a surge of interest in the sport. The American Canoe Association supervises competition in this country.

BACKPACKING

Desolation Valley in northern California used to be one of the loneliest, most beautiful spots on earth. But one summer day in 1972, 2,688 people visited Desolation Valley. It's not so desolate there any more.

The headlong rush to escape the Establishment and the ever-growing need many people feel to get away from the polluted air and crowding of the cities have sent millions upon millions of young people into the remote lakes and valleys of North America. Sophisticated lightweight equipment has contributed to the surge, and freeze-dried foods have been a factor. Would you believe that your teen-age son can cook up a kettle of turkey tetrazzini in the remotest forest wilderness in about ninety seconds?

Youngsters know well the benefits that can be derived from hiking and camping. The first is relaxation. A boy or girl whose role in life is that of a student needs to take time out as much as does an adult who goes to a daily job. Dr. Daniel Henning of Eastern Montana College recently determined that the prime benefit of being in the back country, the wilderness, was one of stress removal, and it applied no matter the age or vocation of the camper. There are aesthetic values, too, the sights and sounds and the "feel" of nature.

Backpacking

To many young people, hiking and camping represent a new reality, a fresh set of challenges. Being able to meet these challenges successfully gives a young person a distinct sense of achievement. "I *never* thought I could walk twenty-five miles in a day," a young college student exclaimed to Dr. Henning.

GETTING STARTED

If your child is a pre-teen-ager, introduce him to hiking by degrees. Your first outing can be in a city park. Perhaps it will last only an hour or two. Then begin lengthening the walks. Pack along a snack or your lunch.

Overnight trips come next. Many state parks provide lean-tos, A-frame cabins, or similar shelters in which you can bed down. If you don't know how much hiking and camping you'll be doing in the future, you can rent much of the equipment you need. Don't try anything more ambitious than a week-long trip during your first season.

There's a right way to walk, incidentally. The hiker should point his toes straight ahead on every step, coming down lightly on his heel and reaching forward with his toes to push off. There should be spring in the ankle on each step. That's why it's important to keep your feet parallel to the direction in which you're heading; slant them to the left or right and you won't be able to get sufficient ankle-spring.

You should also get your hips into each stride. Doing so will add two or three inches to the length of each stride. The idea is to swivel your hips forward with each step. If you've ever seen a walking race, you know what I mean. Of course, competitors in these events exaggerate the hip swivel; essentially, however, it is this type of action that you should seek to develop.

Once on the trail, you shouldn't hurry, but you shouldn't be lackadaisical either. Establish a pace that the group as a whole can maintain throughout the day. Schedule sufficient rest stops, perhaps one that's ten minutes in length for every fifty minutes on the trail. When you do stop, be sure the youngsters relax. Have each remove his pack and stretch out.

The pace that you set during the day should be such that you arrive at your campsite tired—but not exhausted. You and the other members of your party should have the strength and energy to enjoy the tasks involved in preparing camp.

It's usually best to put the faster hikers at the end of the line, slower ones in front. Otherwise, the slow walkers lag behind, and you can wind up having your group strewn out over a mile or two of trail. If there is a wide discrepancy in ages and hiking skill among the members of your group, divide it into two sections. In the morning, the slower hikers leave camp first; the faster boys stay behind to break camp—take down the tents, burn rubbish, etc. (Being faster hikers means that they are probably older and stronger boys, and thus better able to carry the tents and other equipment.) The day's hike can be scheduled so that both sections arrive at the next campsite at about the same time. Or, if you want to even up the delegation of chores, you can arrange for the slower section to arrive first and begin gathering firewood, hauling water, etc.

Even though you seek to establish an even pace throughout the day, your party will cover more ground in the morning hours because they're fresher and it's likely to be cooler. It's best to break camp after a leisurely breakfast, allowing time for the sun to dry out the tents.

Ten miles is about the distance you can expect to cover, although it depends on the skill and experience of your hikers and the type of terrain you're covering. Plan to have lunch at the seven- or eight-mile point. You should arrive at the night's campsite at about three in the afternoon. This will leave plenty of time for preparing dinner, doing laundry and other chores, and also for recreational pursuits like fishing and photography. Campers should be in bed not long after dark.

One of your most important responsibilities as group leader is the selection of each night's campsite. Many trail maps designate camp-sites, which simplifies your task. You want a campsite that features level land with good drainage and the availability of pure water. If you're not packing along a camp stove, a supply of firewood is another ne-cessity. It's also good to have shade in the afternoon and direct sunlight in the morning. You'll have to make some compromises, however; a perfect campsite is almost impossible to find.

As leader, you'll also be responsible for the preparation of meals, or at least for their planning. This should be done weeks before the hike. Freeze-dried foods, which you can buy at any camping equip-ment store, have revolutionized the art of outdoor cookery. "Just add water and heat," say the directions on the food packet. It's really not much more difficult than that.

In the weeks preceding your first major outing, begin to prepare an equipment list. What you take will depend on the number of hikers in your group, the duration of the trip, the time of the year, and your own personal preferences. Use the list to check off each item as you pack.

164

Backpacking

Naturally, you want to keep weight to a minimum. Some back-packers are especially diligent in this regard, and will even saw off the handle of a toothbrush for the tiny weight reduction it represents. You don't have to go to this extreme, but you should appraise every article carefully as to weight, asking yourself, "Do I really need it?" After your first trip or two, you'll learn to leave behind seldom-used items.

What should a loaded pack weigh? Forty pounds is the absolute maximum for a man in good condition covering level ground. Maybe your youngster can cope with half that amount; maybe not. It depends on his size and strength.

GETTING ASSISTANCE

There are more than a score of organizations ready to give the novice backpacker helpful information and advice on hiking and camping. Some of these sponsor group treks under the supervision of trained guides. It's a good idea for the beginner to travel with someone of experience until he acquires the knowledge and skills that backpacking demands.

One of the most active organizations of this type is the Sierra Club (1050 Mills Tower, 270 Bush St., San Francisco, Calif. 94104), an organization which was founded in 1892 by naturalist John Muir and which now has chapters in eleven states—Arizona, Colorado, Illinois, Michigan, Nevada, New Mexico, New York, Oregon, Texas, Washington, and Wisconsin—and also in Washington, D.C. The club organizes backpacking trips that vary from simple day-long hikes to what are referred to as a "High Trip," backpacking adventures of several days' duration over mountainous terrain at altitudes of about 9,000 feet.

The Sierra Club publishes an extensive list of authoritative books and pamphlets covering virtually every aspect of hiking and camping. One, titled *Food for Knapsackers,* is regarded as the definitive book on the subject. Write to the Sierra Club and request a free book list.

For hikers in the eastern United States, there's the Appalachian Trail Conference (1718 N St., N.W., Washington, D.C. 20036), a federation of thirty-three hiking clubs which support the 2050-mile Maine-to-Georgia Appalachian Trail, the longest continuously marked trail in the world. Like the Sierra Club, the Appalachian Trail Conference has available helpful booklets on a variety of backpacking topics.

Many thousands of hikers and campers in the Northeast belong to the New York–New Jersey Trail Conference (G.P.O. Box 2250, New York, N.Y. 10001), an organization that maintains over 700 miles of trails in the states of New York and New Jersey.

Other regional or national organizations that are active in this field include: American Youth Hostels (Delaplane, Va. 22025), the Federation of Western Outdoor Clubs (201 S. Ashdale St., West Covina, Calif. 91790), and the National Campers and Hikers Association (7172 Transit Rd., Buffalo, N.Y. 14221), which describes itself as the "oldest, largest, and fastest-growing family camping organization in North America." The association has close to five hundred local chapters and provides members with information on local roads, trails and campsites.

Any backpacker, whether novice or experienced, has to learn all that he possibly can about the terrain and climate of the area that he plans to visit. When it comes to the matter of terrain, the way to become informed is by means of the topographical maps prepared and distributed by the U.S. Geological Survey. These give information as to the character of the land in rich detail.

Maps of this type are published in sections that the Geological Survey refers to as "quadrangles." Write to the U.S. Geological Survey (GSA Building, Washington, D.C. 20242) and request an index to the topographical maps for the state or general area in which you are interested. This will enable you to order the quadrangles you need. Each costs about 75¢. Quadrangle maps are also sold at each of the several regional offices of the Geological Survey, at most National Forest or National Park Headquarters (listed in your telephone directory under "U.S. Government, Agriculture Department" in the case of the Forest Service or "Interior Department" in the case of National Parks), or at local map retailers (listed in the Yellow Pages under "Maps").

Maps for Canada, similar to USGS maps, can be obtained through the Map Distribution Office of the Department of Mines and Technical Surveys (615 Booth St., Ottawa, Ontario). In requesting information, make reference to maps of the National Topographical Series.

To make an evaluation of the weather conditions of an area, the camper can rely on the comprehensive records compiled by the U.S. Weather Bureau. These are summarized in a series of books, one for each state or region of the country, titled *Climatic Summary of the United States, Supplement for 1931 through 1952.* Each one contains a thorough review of past weather conditions, including detailed information as to precipitation, or absence of it, and temperature ranges. The camper can thus make a sensible choice of what to pack. These booklets are available from the Superintendent of Documents (U.S. Government Printing Office, Washington, D.C. 20402). Each costs 20¢ to 70¢.

166

Backpacking

EQUIPMENT

At the outset, most young people purchase an equipment "package" that includes boots, a pack frame and sack, and a sleeping bag. If they find their initial hikes enjoyable, they are then likely to buy a tent, stove and other accessory items. This is according to a survey conducted by Dr. J. W. Kilpatrick, Jr., of California State University, the results of which appeared recently in *Better Camping* magazine.

Be sure that the young camper does his buying at a store where the salespeople have some expertise. Most novices need an experienced person to assist them. Have the youngster become as knowledgeable as he can about equipment before he makes his buying decisions. One way to become informed is by studying catalogs. Here is a list of some of the companies that send free catalogs on request:

Alpine Designs, 6185 East Arapahoe St., Boulder, Colo. 80303
Camp & Trail Outfitters, 21 Park Pl., New York, N.Y. 10007
Camp Trails, 4111 West Clarendon Ave., Phoenix, Ariz. 85063
Gerry Division of Outdoor Sports Industries, Inc., 5450 North Valley Highway, Denver, Colo. 80216
Kelty Pack, 10909 Tuxford St., Sun Valley, Calif. 91352
Trailblazer by Winchester, Taylorsville Rd., Statesville, N.C. 28677

Boots. Every backpacker should wear one-piece, full-grain-leather, lug-soled trail boots. The young hiker in your family is undoubtedly capable of tramping several miles wearing sneakers or so-called Sahara boots, but such footwear is foolhardy. A foot blister in the wilderness is about as welcome as three days of rain. Ankle-high trail boots help to prevent such problems, and they also protect the feet against cuts or bruises that can be sustained when you're crossing rock-strewn terrain. They keep out cold and dampness, too.

Buy your youngster a boot that is leather-lined and has a sturdy appearance. Plan to pay about $40. Look for double-stitched reverse-welt construction, a full steel shank, and a heavy-duty sole, at least a half-inch thick. Look for boots with a scree guard and an overlap closure; both work to keep pebbles out and even grains of sand. Hooks or zippers can cause problems. Get a boot with a simple and efficient lace system.

Boots should fit snugly, but the toes should be able to move freely. When buying boots, unlace one and slide the foot forward until the toes touch the front. At the other end, between the back of the heel

167

and the boot, there should be a gap wide enough for you to wedge in a finger.

Once the boot is laced and tied, there should be no movement at all in the heel area, not side to side nor up and down, nor should the foot be able to slide forward. Test the boots by having the child walk around the store for several minutes.

If there is no store that sells quality boots in your area, you may want to deal with a mail-order supplier. In such a case, don't send him merely the shoe size of the young camper you're equipping. Instead, trace an outline of the feet being fitted and send it along with the order.

Boots should be broken in before they are worn on a long hike. They should be worn around the house on the weekends, on trips to the supermarket, or on walks in the park. Some experts recommend soaking new boots in water, donning them, lacing them tightly, and then walking about until they dry. What happens is that the leather conforms to the shape of the foot. But don't try this with cheap boots.

If, during the breaking-in period, the stitching in the boot bottom chafes the feet, cover the bottom with an insole, which you can buy in shoe-repair shops or a drugstore. Be sure it's made of perforated nylon or plastic; felt or foam rubber cause perspiration and, eventually, cold feet.

168

Backpacking

It's not only boots that need breaking in; feet do, too. If your youngster is a novice hiker, have him give his feet an alcohol rub each day in the week preceding his first outing. This will help to toughen them.

A blister can be something of a catastrophe. But if you take the time to get well-fitting quality boots and break them in properly, you can help prevent a blister from occurring. Once on the trail, the hiker should always stop at the first sign of foot soreness. Get the boot off and examine the foot to find out what's wrong. Cover any reddened area with a piece of moleskin plaster.

Pack frames and bags. The pack frame is designed to ride high on the shoulders by means of a pair of wide and padded straps, while a waistbelt acts to transfer part of the weight of the load to the hips. Pack frames come in many sizes and styles. Kelty Pack, one of the leading firms in the field, offers four sizes, ranging from small ("for persons of slight physique who expect to carry small, light loads") to large ("for persons of heavy physique who expect to carry big, heavy loads").

Have the young hiker try out several sizes and styles until he finds one that seems suitable. Among the features that you should look for are shoulder straps with tabler buckles which allow adjustment when the pack is in place, a contoured backband which will conform to the wearer's back under the pressure of the load, and permanent studs, not loose pins, to hold the pack to the frame. In the case of a frame meant to carry a really heavy load, over 40 pounds, say, look for an extra V-shaped bar welded into the frame top; it's meant to give added support and thus increase stability.

Fit is the most important item of all, however. The size frame a person needs depends on the length of his torso as measured along the backbone from the base of the neck to the waist at hipbone level. The greater this distance, the longer the pack frame should be. The best test as to whether a pack is going to be comfortable or not is how straight the wearer can stand with the loaded pack on his back. If he is forced to lean forward it's a sign the frame doesn't fit well. As all of this probably suggests, the only way to assure proper fit is to test-wear the frame and the pack under a mock load. If the store that you plan to deal with doesn't provide this service, shop elsewhere.

As for the pack bag, it should be made of water-repellent (none are really "waterproof"), abrasion-resistant woven nylon or military-specification duck. All zippers should be covered. The bag should be constructed in such a way that the wearer can so organize the load

169

that even when the bag is half empty the weight remains concentrated high on his shoulders. The bag should have several compartments or pockets which permit the hiker to find oft-needed items without disturbing the entire load. Camp Trails, the firm that developed the aluminum pack frame, offers an "extendable" bag, which permits the user to pack along extra bulky gear, like the additional gear needed for cold-weather camping, without the need of a frame extension.

Sleeping bags. The type of sleeping bag purchased depends to a great extent on where the party is going to do its camping—that is, the climate or, especially, the coldness of the nights. Warmth implies comfort, and after a day of hiking, fishing or exploring, the young camper, or *any* camper, wants a big serving of comfort.

Sleeping bags are often described as being such and such "cut size" or "finished size." Cut size refers to the dimensions of the cover before the bag is stitched; finished size is the completed size, after the bag has been sewn together. If you are buying a bag for someone who is taller than average, you may need a bag of extra length, but otherwise the matter of length will be no problem.

Today's young hikers and backpackers prefer "mummy" bags, those with a tapered shape and drawstring hood. In terms of warmth for weight, the mummy bag is a great deal more efficient than the rectangular bag that is popular with family campers.

Down, prime northern goose down, is the best insulation ever discovered for a sleeping bag. What makes it so good is its loft, its ability to create a great thickness—dead air space—in relation to its weight. In addition, down is compressible, which means it can be packed into a small space. It is also light, soft and odorless.

About the only fault that you can find with down is that some people are allergic to it. If your young camper is, buy a bag with manmade insulation, like Dacron. The trouble with manmade fibers is that they're somewhat heavier and much less compressible than down, so they pack less efficiently.

Remember the old patchwork quilts? They consisted of two layers of fabric with cotton, wool or feathers in between. They had crisscross stitching to prevent the filler from balling up in the corners. Well, sleeping bags, within their outer shell, have similar stitching, and for the same reason. There are several different types. The one to avoid is the box-baffle type. Quilts were sewn in this fashion, straight through front to back, and as a result there was no insulation at the stitch points. This is no great problem in a quilt but when a sleeping bag is put together like this it can result in cold spots.

170

What to look for is overlapping or slant-baffle stitching. In either of these, the opposing stitch points are offset from one another; there are no stitched-through areas, no cold spots.

Zippers are a matter of personal preference. A zipper down the side makes a bag easy to get in and out of, but it adds to the weight and to the cost, and unless the zipper is fitted with an efficient overlap warmed air can leak out.

To go with the sleeping bag, you will have to buy a foam pad to serve as a ground cover. No one sleeps on the bare ground any more. A pad costs about $10.

Tents. What is usually needed is a ridgepole tent of plastic-coated nylon with a zippered storm curtain, jointed aluminum poles,

pre-rigged nylon guy lines, and a waterproof nylon fly that "floats" over the tent proper to prevent condensation inside.

The tent size depends on how many people are to be in the party. One rule of thumb states that the tent should be large enough to provide about 14 square feet of floor space for each person. The height should be such that it enables you to sit up without striking your head.

The camper should know how the tent pitches before he makes his purchase. When trading at a store that sells camping equipment exclusively, the dealer is likely to have several tents set up on the showroom floor. If so, you'll be able to climb inside and get a clear idea of how big each one is and how well constructed. It's really the only way to be able to make a wise decision.

Camp stoves. Some campers like to cook over an open fire, disdaining the use of a camp stove, but be aware that fewer and fewer backpackers are following this policy. The reason is that today's camp stoves are so remarkably efficient and light in weight. Using a stove means there's no time spent hunting for wood, no fussing to get the fire going. What many people are doing is using a stove to prepare camp meals, then at nightfall building a campfire for warmth and pleasure.

Of course, the type of stove purchased will pretty much depend on how many people there are in the camping party. Optimus, Inc.

172

Backpacking

(P. O. Box 3848, 652 East Commonwealth, Fullerton, Calif. 92634) sells a gas-burning stove called the Svea that's about the size of a small coffeepot. Made of brass and aluminum, it weighs only one and one-half pounds. It can boil an egg in six minutes. But it's hardly practical for group feeding. However, Optimus makes a variety of other models, as does the Coleman Company (Wichita, Kansas 67201), the leading American manufacturer of camp stoves. Optimus is a Swedish firm.

While most backpackers prefer gas-burning stoves, there is a demand for stoves that use propane or butane as a fuel. They light instantly and the fuel is cleaner-burning than gasoline. A (disposable) cartridge of fuel, purchased in a sporting goods store, lasts from two and a half to three hours and weighs about 12 ounces. The Primus-Sievert Company (354 Sackett Point Rd., North Haven, Conn. 06472) is a leading manufacturer of propane-powered camp stoves. This firm and the others mentioned in this section will send you free catalogs.

Clothing. Clothing for warm-weather hiking should permit a free flow of air through the cloth so that excess body heat will be carried away by air currents. Actually, what is worn on summertime hikes is only to protect from the sun and underbrush.

In cold weather, several layers of lightweight clothing are better than one heavy outer layer. The idea is for the clothing to retain the body's heat but at the same time permit the evaporation of perspiration. No one should go without a wool hat.

Socks. Many experts advise wearing two pairs of socks, an inner lightweight pair of nylon or other polyester, and an outer pair of wool. This system helps keep the feet dry and protects them against boot friction.

BOOKS AND PUBLICATIONS

The Complete Walker (Alfred A. Knopf, $7.95), by Colin Fletcher, is the standout book in this field. The author is an inveterate backpacker who has been confronted by every problem the activity can possibly present, and he sets down his solutions in careful detail, writing with charm and enthusiasm.

Nelson's Encyclopedia of Camping (Thomas Nelson and Co., $7.50), by E. C. Janes, covers a wide range of topics of interest to the family camper. *The Hikers' and Backpackers' Handbook* (Winchester Press, $5.95), by W. K. Merrill, is an authoritative guide; the author is a retired National Park ranger.

The U.S. Department of the Interior has available a score or more of booklets covering various aspects of outdoor recreation in the National Parks. These include: "Back-Country Travel in the National Park System" (35¢); "Camping in the National Park System" (25¢); "National Forest Wilderness and Primitive Area" (15¢); and "Outdoor Recreation in the National Forests" (60¢). Order from the Superintendent of Documents (U.S. Government Printing Office, Washington, D.C. 20402).

The surge of popularity in backpacking has brought many novices upon the scene. Inexperienced backpackers often make these mistakes:

○ *They carry too heavy a load.*

○ *They expect their wives, or girl friends, to carry too heavy a load.*

○ *They leave behind needed items.*

○ *They plan too ambitious a trip the first time out.*

—Dick Kelty
President
Kelty Pack Company

FISHING

A really serious fisherman might prefer this chapter to be titled "Angling." "Fishing" can be catching fish without regard to tactics. "Angling" is much different. It involves special equipment and well-thought-out strategy.

A small child can be taught to "fish" in about eleven seconds. The only equipment required is a length of line and a hook—you don't even need a rod. Onto the hook goes natural bait—a worm, insect, grub or crayfish. The baited hook lies still beneath the surface until a fish bites.

There's not the slightest doubt that "fishing" is fun, and it even offers moments of high excitement. But "angling" is *more* fun and can provide far greater thrills—and, thanks to modern equipment, it's not difficult to learn.

Angling, to a large degree, is casting. To make a cast, the angler uses his rod to "throw" live bait or an artificial lure over the water, which he then retrieves, hoping to attract a fish as the line is drawn in. It is generally agreed that it is much more sporting to catch a fish by casting.

There are many types of casting: bait casting, fly casting and spin casting for freshwater fish, and surf casting in salt water. Beginners often experience difficulties in bait casting and fly casting. Such casting is tricky; it involves a quick wrist snap. The beginner often has trouble in timing the backcast and starting the rod forward neither too soon nor not soon enough, and the result is that he loses the fly or even ends up hooking himself.

Spin casting, however, is another matter. Spin casting refers to casting with a reel in which the spool within remains stationary. The entire unit is enclosed in a plastic or metal shell. When the rod is whipped forward, the line spins out without any drag, without any restraint, a system that eliminates backlash.

Using a spin-casting outfit, a youngster can learn to make long and accurate casts with a minimum of practice time. The growing popularity and widespread use of spin-casting equipment doesn't mean that bait casting and fly casting have gone the way of the buggy whip. Not at all. Greater accuracy is possible with bait casting, and bigger fish can be handled more easily. The bait caster has more control over his line when "playing" a fish, and snag-infested waters are less troublesome for him. But for the beginner, spin casting is the best method, the one that he will master with the greatest speed. Later, as his interest and skill build, he can learn to use other types of equipment.

To go with the spinning reel, choose a lightweight 6-foot rod. Fill the spool with a 6-pound-test line to within $1/16$ to $1/8$ inch of the spool's outer edge. Failing to fill the spool sufficiently or overfilling it can cause the line to stick.

Don't start the youngster casting right away. Give him time to become familiar with the mechanics of the reel. One good way to introduce him to the equipment is to take him boat fishing. Rig his line with a No. 8 wire hook and sliding sinker. After attaching the sinker, pinch a BB shot sinker onto the line about 18 inches from the hook to prevent the larger sinker from sliding to the hook. Use live bait, worms or crawlers.

Once you've positioned the boat over the area you'll be fishing, instruct him to hold his rod naturally, his forefinger around the finger hook, his thumb on the push-button. He should turn his wrist so the reel's crank side is up. This may seem awkward to him at first, but later, when he begins casting, this positioning will enable him to get greater wrist action into the cast, which means more distance, more accuracy. The reel's non-reverse lever, if it has one, should be in the off position.

Fishing

Have him press the pushbutton, dropping the line, sinker and bait over the side. When the sinker hits bottom and the line becomes slack, have him turn the handle half a turn to engage the reel. Then row or drift, allowing the sinker to drag on the bottom. "How will I know when I have a fish?" he is likely to ask. "Don't worry," you can tell him, "you'll know." And he will.

Once the youngster has taken a few fish using this simple technique, he should be thoroughly familiar with the mechanics of the spin-casting outfit; he will have the "feel" of it. He can then be schooled in the technique of the overhand cast. Demonstrate it several times before you allow him to try. Using your thumb, press down on the pushbutton, bring the rod back smartly and then forward without pausing. When the lure or baited hook is traveling at maximum speed, release the push button, shooting the lure toward the target. It won't take many tries for the youngster to get the hang of it.

SPIN-CASTING EQUIPMENT

When purchasing a spin-casting outfit, there are certain things to look for. Generally, buy a unit of sturdy construction. The reel should be simple to disassemble for cleaning and oiling.

The reel spool should be machined aluminum; avoid plastic spools. Inquire as to whether replacement spools are available.

Turn the handle to assure that it operates easily. Look for a non-reverse clutch control, a small lever mounted on one side of the housing which, when set, prevents the handle or crank from flying backward when a fish is hooked.

Examine the line pick-up mechanism to be certain that there is no chance of line-pinching. The pick-up itself should be made of metal.

Rods. The rods used in spin casting are almost always made of tubular fiberglass, and are usually classed as being extra-light, light or medium. They are generally longer than bait-casting rods—6, 6½, or 7 feet. Bait rods range from 4½ to 6½ feet. The added length means that a lighter lure—or live bait—can be thrown farther and with greater ease. Lightweight, whippy tips, which reduce the pull on the line when a fish is hooked, are another feature of spin-casting rods.

The guides (the steel loops through which the line runs) are slightly larger than those on bait-casting rods. Longer spin-casting rods are two-piece and ferrule-joined. Sometimes the shorter rods are metal and telescope for easy carrying and storage.

177

Line and lures. Monofilament line, as opposed to braided line, is best for spin casting. The line's breaking strength is determined by the type of fishing you are going to be doing. For example, for perch, trout or bluegill, a 4- to 6-pound-test line is recommended; for bigger fish—bass, pickerel or northern pike—you need 8- to 12-pound-test.

Spin-casting rods will handle lures up to one ounce without difficulty, but they operate with the greatest efficiency when lighter lures—⅛ to ⅝ ounce—are being used.

Molded-rubber lures are excellent for use with spin-casting rods. A spoon, which is similar in shape to the bowl of the spoon, can also be effective. Experiment with spoons of different types.

SALTWATER FISHING

The condition of surf encountered along the Atlantic, Pacific and Gulf coasts covers a wide range, and the type of fishing varies too. Surfcasters in New Jersey and Long Island fish for flounder, bluefish, kingfish and striped bass. Farther to the south, it's seatrout, sailfish and Spanish mackerel. In the Pacific Northwest, salmon is likely to be the object. It can be barracuda and corbina in Southern California.

While it is not easy to make general statements as to equipment, one thing can be said with certainty: there is a continuing trend toward the use of light equipment. Actually, most freshwater gear is suitable for saltwater fishing.

Of course, rod and reel manufacturers do make spinning rods and reels designed especially for saltwater use. In the light-tackle class, the rod ranges from 6 to 7½ feet in length. The reel, in the case of a young beginner, should weigh from 8 to 10 ounces. If he uses anything heavier, the continuous casting may tire him. The monofilament line should test at 6, 8, 10 or 12 pounds. Almost any lure that weighs from ¼ to 1½ ounces can be used. Have the youngster become familiar with a few basic types.

Can spin-casting equipment be used in salt water? The answer is yes, but a qualified yes. You have to have a corrosion-proof reel or be willing to give the reel regular cleaning and oiling to protect it.

OTHER TYPES OF FISHING

A youngster can become skilled in fly fishing—if he practices. The trick is to put the fly just where you want it, and since the fly itself has almost no weight, it is the weight of the line itself that is used for casting. Usually two or more false casts, with the line whipping back

and forth without touching the water, are necessary to get enough line out. Have the youngster practice casting in the backyard (without a fly). He should be able to achieve good distance and accuracy before he tries the technique at a stream or pond.

Selecting the proper fly takes practice, too. Bear in mind that the quarry in fly fishing is a surface feeder. See what the fish are eating, then offer them something that's comparable to it.

Surf casting can be done with any type of tackle, but heavy surf gear is required when the waves are high. Fish feed at the first line of breakers, so you have to get the lure or baited hook just beyond.

The surf-casting rod has a tip that is 6 to 7 feet long. It attaches to a hardwood handle that is 28 to 32 inches long. Surf-casting reels have wide spools that hold at least 200 yards of line. Obviously, this type of equipment demands that the user be of good size and strength.

Big-game fishing is done mostly from charter boats, with tackle, bait and general advice provided by the boat captain. It's a good way to introduce a youngster to saltwater tackle, since your only investment is the day's charter fee, from $50 to $100, depending on the location and season.

Party boats operate on regular schedules from port cities, taking fishermen to offshore fishing grounds. Sometimes they are called "open boats," because they're "open" to anyone who has the fee. This can range from $5 to $25, depending on the area, length of the trip, and the amount and type of equipment provided.

LICENSES

For most freshwater fishing, a state fishing license is required. These are usually available at county courthouses, town halls, and, in some states, at fishing-tackle shops. The fees for licenses range from $1 to $5 for residents and from $2 to $15 for nonresidents. Generally, no license is required for saltwater angling, but there are exceptions.

Virtually all states have established open and closed seasons on the various types of fish within their borders. Be sure the season is open on the species you're hoping to catch.

To obtain information on this subject, write the conservation department of the state where you plan to fish. Simply address your letter to the state capital. Request a copy of the state's fishing laws, including information about licenses and open and closed seasons. You can also ask for information on where the best fishing is to be found, and for travel information.

ORGANIZATIONS

The American Casting Association (P. O. Box 51, Nashville, Tenn. 37202) is the most active of the several angling organizations devoted to sportsmanship, competition and conservation. A federation of about fifty local clubs and state and regional associations, the ACA promotes casting not only as a recreational activity but also as a competitive sport, sanctioning local and state tournaments and sponsoring an annual national tournament. The organization also provides instruction through workshops and clinics. Write for information concerning activities the ACA may sponsor in your area.

The International Spin Fishing Association (P. O. Box 81, Downey, Calif. 90241), a federation of individuals and sportsmen's clubs, registers records made on spinning tackle and presents annual awards in several spin-fishing categories. The Association of Surf Angling (851 Norway Ave., Trenton, N.J. 08629) promotes the conservation of saltwater fish and game and also supervises and sanctions surf-casting tournaments.

Fishing

For women, there's the International Women's Fishing Association (P. O. Box 2025, Miami Beach, Fla. 33480), which promotes a variety of tournaments for sportfisherwomen. The Sport Fishing Institute (719 Thirteenth St. N.W., Washington, D.C. 20005) is a conservation organization supported by equipment manufacturers. It publishes periodic reviews of both government and private conservation activities.

BICYCLING

The bicycle boom which began in 1960 continues almost unabated, and an estimated 75 million Americans now own bikes. Which is fine, because physical fitness experts rank cycling as close to ideal as a conditioning exercise.

"The aerobic benefits to the internal organs from cycling," says Dr. Kenneth Cooper in *Aerobics,* "are identical with those of running and swimming." If your youngster wants to take up bicycling, whether it be merely for utilitarian purposes, such as running errands and going to the tennis courts, or something much more ambitious, like cycle touring, which implies visiting surrounding neighborhoods or adjacent towns or even distant ones, by all means encourage him. Buy him a bike, a sleek ten-speeder if he wants it. It could be the best investment you will ever make toward his good health.

Physical fitness is the principal reason for the tremendous surge in the purchase and use of bicycles. Dr. Paul Dudley White, the eminent heart specialist who was once described as having done more for bicycling than any other person, spoke frequently about the benefits of the sport, and what he said is worth noting. "Electric can openers and toothbrushes, garbage disposals, automobiles with power steering, the hypnotic TV set," he declared, "all have made our lives easier and more pleasant and all have conspired to cut to almost nothing the

Bicycling

amount of physical effort required to live in the twentieth century. Regularly and properly used, the bicycle can be a marvelous antitoxin to the poison of living this too-easy life.

"First and foremost, riding a bicycle is fun. Equally important, however, is the established fact that cycling is good for you. It's a good aid to muscle tone. It aids circulation of the blood and promotes proper breathing. A nightly pre- or post-dinner bicycle ride aids digestion, helps weight control and promotes sound, relaxing sleep."

The interest in ecology has also been a factor in the growing popularity of the bicycle. As one manufacturer points out, it is the only form of transportation—including the horse—that doesn't pollute.

A third factor is the encouragement for the bicycle that has come from municipal, state and federal programs. According to the Bicycle Institute of America, 6,300 miles of bicycle paths have been laid in 200 cities. A law recently enacted in Oregon permits a portion of gasoline and road-use revenues to be used for the construction of bicycle paths.

An often overlooked reason for cycling's mushrooming popularity is a technological one: the ten-speed lightweight bicycle. Once a youngster of thirteen or fourteen tries out one of these, it will be hard to get him on any other kind.

BUYING A BIKE

Buy from a bicycle dealer, not a department store and not a discount store. The usual reason applies—you'll be buying from a more knowledgeable person—but there's another factor. Bicycles are usually shipped from the factory disassembled. At a discount or department store, they're usually put together by salesclerks. The brakes may be poorly adjusted; the wheels may be out of line. Or the store may sell the bike only partly assembled, leaving you to complete the job.

A bicycle dealer, on the other hand, has one or more mechanics on staff to do assembly work. And later, should a minor mechanical problem happen to develop, the bike can be ridden or taken to the shop for adjustment.

If you're thinking that you might be able to save money by buying a used bicycle, forget it. The secondhand market is practically nonexistent, especially in the case of ten-speed models. Dealers have all they can do to fill orders for new bikes.

It's always wise to buy a quality bike, because the price you pay can be prorated over several years. A cheap bike isn't going to last more than a year or two.

To determine a quality product, look for tipoffs in the way the bike has been manufactured. The frame of a quality bike is made of three distinct metal tubes, which are soldered into lugs at the connecting point. A mediocre bike has no such lugs. The tubes look as if they have been inserted into one another.

The very best bike frames are made of Reynolds high-strength steel, but not all Reynolds frames are of superior quality. Look for a label that says "Guaranteed built with Reynolds '531' butted tubes, forks and stays." (The term "butted tubes" means that the tube metal is heavier at the ends, where one tube joins another and the greatest stress occurs.) This indicates a frame of the very highest quality.

The decal may also say, "Guaranteed built with Reynolds '531' plain gauge tubes, forks and stays." As you can judge, "plain gauge tubes" are not as desirable as butted ones. A label that says simply "Reynolds '531' frame tubing" also damns with faint praise.

Finally, a label that says "Guaranteed built with Reynolds '531' butted frame tubes" should imply to you that, while the tubing is of sufficient quality, the manufacturer skimped on the forks and stays.

Spokes give you an indication of quality, too. Check to see that each is double-butted—that is, that there is a slight increase in spoke circumference toward each end, which makes for added spoke strength. Pluck the spokes as you would the strings of a harp. They should all emit the same musical tone. Any variation means that there is a lack of uniform tightness. A loose spoke can cause a wheel to loose its roundness.

Count the number of spokes. Bikes for young children, those having 10- to 20-inch wheels, should have 28 spokes in each wheel. Any fewer than that number is likely to mean that the bike lacks in strength and hence in durability.

A three-speed English touring model should have 32 spokes in the front wheel and 40 in the rear. Other lightweight models should have 32 or 36 spokes in the front wheel and 36 spokes in the rear.

When it comes to handlebars, there are two different types: what are called "flat" handlebars and the dropped or turned-down type. Flat handlebars are used on coaster-brake and three-speed bicycles. They permit the rider to sit upright as he pedals. High-riser handlebars, which position the hands at about chin level, are a variation of the flat type.

Turned-down handlebars are usual for ten-speed derailleur lightweight bicycles and for single-speed fixed-gear bicycles that are used in track racing. There are several variations of the turned-down type, but each one serves to position the cyclist at about a 45° angle. This

Bicycling

not only helps him to use his leg muscles with greater efficiency but cuts down wind resistance, and both factors, of course, are crucial to competitive cycling.

A recent study by *Consumer Guide* found narrow leather saddles to be more comfortable than the wider spring-mattress type. The latter type chafes the inside of the rider's thighs. In addition, the springs of the mattress saddle absorb some of the power of the pedal stroke. It takes more energy to get where you're going.

Getting the right fit. In bikes for young children, fit relates to the size of the wheel, which varies from 10 to 20 inches in diameter. Beginning at about nine or ten, a boy or girl is usually big enough to handle a bike with a 26-inch wheel. Bikes of this variety come in different frame sizes, from 19 to 24 inches. (There are also children's bikes with 22- and 24-inch wheels, but most youngsters make the switch from their first bike to the 26-incher without an intermediate stop.) Frame size is determined by measuring the long metal tube into which the seat fits, called the seat tube, from top to bottom. If the tube is 22 inches long, then the entire frame is said to be a 22-inch frame.

Have the youngster straddle the top tube, the horizontal tube that extends from the handlebars to the seat. Both his feet should be flat to the ground as he straddles. Buy him the biggest frame size that he can straddle comfortably. Another rule of thumb says that the frame size of a rider's bike should be 9 to 10 inches less than his inseam measurement.

Once you've found a frame size that is suitable, the next step is to adjust the saddle height. A surprising number of cyclists ride on saddles that are too low for efficient pedaling. They get tired quickly—and they don't know why. Have your youngster sit on the saddle. With one leg straight and the related pedal at six o'clock, his heel should just touch the pedal.

Once the seat height has been established, try this test. Have the child sit on the saddle while the bike is standing. He should be just able to touch the floor with his toes. If he can put his feet flat to the floor, the saddle is too low. If he's unbalanced and keeps tilting from one side to the other, the saddle is too high.

Once the seat level is set, you can adjust the handlebars. In the case of the flat type, raise the center post until the horizontal bar is on the same level as the nose of the saddle. Then tilt the handlebars forward slightly. These are only general recommendations, however. Other modifications to suit the rider will probably be necessary.

What is said above also applies to dropped handlebars. But here again the rider has to decide for himself what "feels right." It's pretty much a trial-and-error process.

Sizes and styles. For a child of five or six, buy a balloon-tire bicycle with 10- to 20-inch wheels and a coaster brake. The coaster brake is especially important. A small child doesn't have the hand strength to operate hand-lever caliper brakes; he needs the type you operate by back-pedaling. Many people feel that training wheels—small wheels on either side of the rear wheel—should never be used because they prevent the child from learning to balance himself. If you do use them, the child should be able to discard them in three or four weeks, depending on how much riding he does.

Bicycling

Avoid bicycles with high-riser handlebars, those that put the child's hands at about the level of his chin. They make steering difficult, even awkward, and must be considered dangerous.

Buy a good bicycle; pay $45 to $50 for it. Since the seat and handlebars can be raised as the child grows, the bicycle should last several years.

For an older child, age ten to twelve, the so-called English touring model is usually the best. (Despite the name, several American companies make bikes of this type.) It's a good model for day-to-day city riding and short trips in the country.

A bike of this type has 26-inch wheels, with a three-speed rear hub and caliper brakes. Tires are 1⅜ inches in size, with tubes. Select a frame size to suit the youngster's height. They vary from 19 to 24 inches. If the child is going to be using the bike for delivering newspapers or groceries, ask for sturdier tires, ones that are 1¾ inches.

Be sure that the bicycle is equipped with front and rear lights if the youngster is going to be using it after dark. The most practical lights are the generator type. Since they draw their power from the turning wheels, you never have to worry about a battery going dead.

The three-speed touring bike costs from $75 to $100. It will satisfy the youngster who wants a bicycle to travel to and from school or to visit nearby friends. But if your youngster seems destined to become a dedicated cycling enthusiast, and interested in long-distance touring, the bicycle to buy is a ten-speed lightweight model, discussed separately below.

One other kind of bike must be mentioned here. It's the minibike, a small folding bicycle that has 16- or 20-inch wheels. The minibike can easily be taken apart and carried in the trunk of a car, or it can be stored in an apartment closet. But minibikes have several disadvantages. Since the wheels are of relatively small diameter, the rider is close to the ground, and he is unstable as a result, particularly if the bike is ridden on slick pavement or a gravel driveway. The small wheel is also inefficient in terms of power expended related to distance traveled. In other words, bikes of this type are good for only short trips. Finally, experts have criticized minibikes for their lack of efficient brakes.

Once you've made a buying decision, have your youngster road-test the bike to check the brakes and gearing system. With coaster brakes, he should get a pronounced wheel skid. In the case of hand brakes, the brake blocks should apply pressure on the rim sides squarely and evenly. When the hand lever is released, the blocks should be well clear of the sides. You can check these points while the bike is standing still. When test-ridden and the brakes are applied, the bike should come to a smooth stop. Test the front and rear brakes individually. They should be of equal braking ability.

There should be no rattles. The pedals should spin freely.

Examine the bicycle carefully. Spin each wheel. Watch the rim from the side to be sure that it is perfectly round. A surprising number aren't. Check the spin of the tires from the front or rear to be sure there is no side-to-side wobble. Each wheel should come to a gradual stop.

To be sure that the wheel hub is in proper adjustment, try this test. Revolve the wheel until the valve stem is at three o'clock. When you remove your hand, the weight of the valve should move the wheel clockwise. If the wheel fails to move, the hub needs adjusting.

THE TEN-SPEED BIKE

Bikes of this type aren't the most practical in the world. Their thin, light tires sometimes puncture on city streets. The gear mechanism, called the derailleur, which guides the chain from one spocket to the next, can be temperamental. It needs frequent adjustment, and in the case of breakdown a professional repair job.

Bicycles of this type costs from $85 to $200 and even beyond. But neither the price nor the problems have seemed to hurt the popularity of bikes of this kind. They have outsold all others in recent years.

Speed is the principal reason. Their light weight—as little as 22 pounds—wide gear range, narrow tires and precision bearings enable 10-speeders to move far faster than the balloon-tired model you rode as a kid. I know of an eight-year-old girl who, one month after she learned to ride and shift one of these bikes, cycled 66 miles in two days. Two years later she pedaled 300 miles with her parents on a week-long hostel trip through Wisconsin.

When buying a ten-speed bike, you should be aware of the difference between most American and European models. With American ten-speeders, particularly those in the lower price range, the gear ratios go from high to low in fairly large jumps. But with European bikes, the gear ratios are closer, because European cyclists are, in the main, more experienced and more physically fit; they do not need extremely low gears.

You can count the teeth in the rear-wheel gears to establish the variations. (The more teeth in a rear-wheel gear, the lower the gearing is.) On a sophisticated European bicycle, the rear-wheel gears are likely to have 23, 21, 19, 17 and 15 teeth. With many American bikes, the count is 28, 24, 20, 17 and 14 teeth. The American gearing is recommended for the young person whose touring is going to include a good deal of hilly terrain. For real mountain climbing—the Rocky Mountains, say—a bike with a 15-speed derailleur system is what's needed.

The gears should get a thorough testing. All gear changes should be accomplished quickly and smoothly. In the case of a derailleur, be alert for spontaneous gear changes that occur while riding, an indication that the gearshift control needs tightening. If the chain "skips" while pedaling, there is not enough chain tension.

If the mechanism is slow to respond or noises result when the rider changes gears, it may mean that the rear gears are not lined up with the tension sprockets.

Before purchasing a new bicycle, especially a sophisticated one, try to get a copy of *Bicycle Buyer's Guide* (Doubleday, $1.95). It contains comprehensive information on all the different bicycles produced by American and foreign manufacturers, with performance ratings and detailed specifications for each.

The Complete Book of Bicycling (Simon and Schuster, $9.95), by Eugene Sloan, contains buying recommendations, too, but is also an informative guide to just about every other aspect of the sport and is particularly good on bike maintenance and repair.

For information on parts and tools for the maintenance and repair of multi-speed bikes, obtain a copy of *The Handbook of Cyclology*. It's available by mail for $2 from Wheel Goods Corporation (14524 21st Ave. North, Minneapolis, Minn. 55441). If you become interested in the history of bicycles or the world of bike racing, an informative and amusingly written book is *Bikes & Riders* (Van Nostrand Reinhold, $7.95), by James Wagenvoord.

PROTECTING A BIKE

Another indication of the bicycle boom is the dramatic upswing in bicycle thefts. A survey of a dozen major cities conducted by the New York *Times* showed a 35 percent increase in thefts in 1972 as compared to the previous year.

"Bike stealing has almost reached the level of organized crime," said the newspaper. "Policemen in this state tell of city-roaming gangs that steal them by the truckload, refurbish them, and sell them for new."

In California in 1971, half a million bikes were stolen, according to an official of the Northern California Bicycle Officers Association. An organized group of thieves stole between 400 and 500 ten-speed bikes in the city of Concord, California, in one year.

What can a young person do to prevent his bike from being stolen? Not very much. He can buy a thick, case-hardened chain and a sturdy lock. But locking the bike merely deters the thief. A good bolt-cutter can snip through a heavy chain with little effort.

The only real solution is to park the bike where a thief can't get at it. A New York bike enthusiast says this: "I never leave my bike. I store it in my living room. If I'm going into a supermarket or a bank, I take the bike with me. If they don't want my bike inside, they don't get my business."

BIKE TOURING

Seeing the country by bike can be one of your youngster's greatest experiences. He or she is certain to get enormous satisfaction out of loading up a pack and riding off with friends on a self-styled adventure. And the physical benefits are enormous, too.

If your youngster is planning on cycle touring, be sure that he or she knows about the American Youth Hostels (Delaplane, Va. 22025), a nonprofit organization whose purpose is "to encourage people of all ages to enjoy the out-of-doors," traveling simply and inexpensively, staying in hostels in the United States and forty-six countries abroad. The term "youth hostels" refers to any overnight accommodation—a school, church, modern building or specially built facility—on a setting that is scenic, historic or cultural. There are about a hundred hostels in the United States and 75,000 people authorized to use them.

The organization has twenty-seven regional councils in the United States, each one of which is made up of smaller AYH clubs. If your youngster joins an AYH cycle-touring group, it will please you to learn that he or she will be supervised by an experienced leader, someone who maps out each day's journey with an understanding of the physical capacity of the individuals in his charge. The group always includes at least one person who is expert in repairing flat tires, broken chains, and the like.

The AYH's *North American Bike Atlas* (Hammond Co., $1.95) maps out in detail a hundred bike tours in every part of the country,

in Canada, Mexico, and the Caribbean. You can order a copy from AYH headquarters. Add 50¢ for postage.

Touring clubs are common in every part of the country. Most are affiliated with the League of American Wheelmen. Sometimes clubs specialize in leisurely Sunday-morning trips, while others emphasize extended treks and regular training. They may hold regular meetings, sponsor a specific number of rides each month, publish newsletters, and, in general, strive to improve bike-riding conditions in their community. Write to the League of American Wheelmen (540 S. Westmont, Whittier, Calif. 90601) for information about clubs in your area. The International Bicycle Touring Society (846 Prospect St., La Jolla, Calif. 92037) is also active in promoting bicycle touring and has available many booklets on the subject.

Touring clubs and park and recreation commissions in many states have stepped up efforts in recent years to attract touring cyclists. The state of New Hampshire publishes and distributes free maps and suggested itineraries for bike trips. It also has available instructions for packing equipment, a digest of state bike regulations, and other helpful information. Many other states provide much the same type of information.

Wisconsin has established a 300-mile bikeway across the state from Kenosha to La Crosse. Ohio encourages cyclists to tour the state's historic Amish country. The "Gold Rush Ride" in California winds through terrain made famous by the Forty-Niners. Maps and background information are available from state tourism offices.

Equipment for bicycle camping should be carried in cycle panniers, which fit over the rear wheel in the same manner pannier packs are slung over the back of a mule or packhorse. Made of conventional pack materials, they often contain plywood stiffeners to prevent them from rubbing against the spokes. For an ambitious, strong-legged youngster, you can get two sets, one for the rear wheel and a smaller set for the front wheel.

Equipment can also be carried in the bike's rear luggage platform, that is, over the rear-wheel panniers. It's a good place for the backpacking tent or the sleeping bag. Equipment can also be lashed to the handlebars or carried in a handlebar basket. However, it is better to carry little or nothing in a handlebar basket; the weight affects the balance of the bike.

The idea in packing a bicycle is to keep the center of gravity as low as possible. You frequently see cyclists wearing backpacks, and big, heavy packs at that, but it's not a wise thing to do. By keeping a low center of gravity, you increase pedaling efficiency.

Using the "ankle" technique of pedaling also contributes to efficiency. Only the ball of the foot should be used, never the arch. This positions the ankle in such a way that the leg muscles power the stroke.

At the top of the stroke, the toe should be pointed upward slightly so as to be able to push the pedal forward and downward. The rider should continue to push after the foot passes the low point of the stroke.

CYCLE COMPETITION

All young bicycle riders race, but few do so in organized competition. What competition does exist is conducted almost entirely by local and state bicycle clubs. There are about 180 of these, each one affiliated with the Amateur Bicycle League of America (611 Orchard Ave., Dearborn, Mich. 48126). The ABL classifies competitors by age: the midget class is for contestants age twelve and younger; intermediates are thirteen to fifteen; and juniors are sixteen to eighteen.

Competitive cycling in Canada is the domain of the Canadian Cycling Association (333 River Rd., Vanier City, Ontario). The organization is also active in promoting bike touring.

Bike racing can take one of several different forms. In the time-trial race, contested over a measured course of 10, 25 or 30 miles, riders compete against the clock. They are started one at a time, a minute apart. The rider with the shortest span of elapsed time wins. In a 25-mile race, a rider would have to be capable of completing the course in 50 to 60 minutes in order to be ranked at the top or near it.

A massed-start race is, as the name implies, conducted like a horserace. The riders start together and the first one across the finish line wins. Races of this type are held on circular park roadways or public highways.

Track racing is limited to the handful of locations in the United States that offer track facilities. They vary in size from indoor board tracks of ten laps to a mile to large outdoor ovals with three laps to the mile. Track racing can take the form of sprint events of 800 or 1,000 meters, or it can be a distance racing, usually 3 or 10 miles.

The Huffman Manufacturing Co. (Dayton, Ohio 45401) has available a booklet titled "A Handbook on Bicycle Tracks and Cycle Racing," which contains useful information on racing equipment and facilities. It's free.

FOR ADDITIONAL INFORMATION

Many organizations (including those mentioned in preceding paragraphs) and business firms are ready to send you free booklets and brochures covering various aspects of cycling. The very best source of information is the Bicycle Institute of America (122 East 42nd St., New York, N.Y. 10017), an organization of manufacturers, wholesalers and retailers of bicycles, parts and accessories. Among the booklets published by the BIA are: "Bicycle Riding Clubs," "Bike Racing on the Campus," "Bikeways," and "Bike Ordinances in the Community." Write for a list of literature and educational materials.

Other sources include The National Safety Council (425 N. Michigan Ave., Chicago, Ill. 60611); U.S. Jaycees (P. O. Box 7, Tulsa, Okla.); and Kemper Insurance Co. (4750 Sheridan Rd., Chicago, Ill. 60640).

VI   COMBATIVE
SPORTS

**WRESTLING
BOXING
JUDO AND KARATE**

WRESTLING

Wrestling, says the dictionary, is a gymnastic exercise between two competitors who attempt to throw each other by grappling. That's what most people think it is, too. But neither the definition nor the prevailing concept of the sport show any appreciation of the fact that wrestling requires a very precise set of skills involving leverage, weight distribution, timing, and countless moves, holds and counterholds.

Quickness; that's the quality coaches look for today. Often a fast man who is lean and wiry is able to overcome a more powerful opponent with apparent ease. Aggressiveness is just as important. A boy has to carry the match to his opponent, and this attitude has to characterize every move that he makes. When he pulls, he must pull hard, as hard as he can. When he squeezes, he has to apply every bit of pressure he can muster. When he moves, he must move quickly and determinedly.

Many coaches believe that wrestling is very much an instinctive sport. Either a youngster is naturally inclined to do well, or he is not.

To some degree, a boy's build determines his wrestling style. A short and stocky youngster is likely to do best when working inside, with underarm and rolling-type holds and counterholds. A tall youngster should develop holds that take advantage of his longer legs and additional body leverage.

The same holds true for the stance, the so-called neutral position. Any position from a low crouch to standing erect is legal. What the stance must do is give complete freedom of movement for a quick offensive thrust, but it must also provide a solid foundation from which to block or counter the move of one's opponent. Most young competitors spread their feet about shoulder-width apart, and put one foot slightly ahead of the other. The knees are slightly bent, the body's weight carried on the balls of the feet. A small boy whose forte is quickness and speed would crouch down low, a stance that enables him to pivot to either the right or left with equal facility.

In high school competition, many of the more punishing and dangerous holds are prohibited. These include the front headlock, straight head scissors, over-scissors, stranglehold, body slam, toe hold, full nelson, and some hammer locks. But there remain literally hundreds of other moves, hold and counterholds that can be used. These include many of the holds in the scissors family, which involve use of the legs. Most holds, of course, are arm holds—the arm lock, chin lock, and those in the nelson family. The young wrestler should become familiar with the various holds and techniques, and select a handful to work on, to master.

WEIGHT DIVISIONS

Because of wrestling's system of weight classification, a youngster

of any size can be successful. In fact, wrestling is one of the few sports in which a smaller youngster can achieve celebrity more quickly than the bigger, taller one, since the small men are usually much quicker and spectators find them more exciting to watch than the heavyweights.

In high school competition, there are twelve weight classes: 98 pounds, 105, 112, 119, 126, 132, 138, 145, 155, 167, 185, and unlimited, in which the minimum weight is 175. To allow for the fact that high school youngsters are growing boys, the weight classifications have some flexibility to them. After January 1, each boy is allowed two extra pounds, and after February 1, one more additional pound. A boy is permitted to compete in one weight class heavier than his own, but in no other.

The weight classification a boy chooses is a critical matter. Often a boy who weighs 150 pounds, say, will pare down his weight so as to be included in the 145-pound class. This, he feels, increases his competitiveness. He realizes that if he goes in the other direction, adding weight until he reaches the 155-pound class, he's not likely to win many matches.

You should help your youngster to decide which weight class is right for him. Most boys who weigh 150 or more can shed 5 pounds without great difficulty, but with smaller boys it can be a problem.

Sometimes a boy makes the mistake of letting his competition

199

influence him in determining his weight classification. He will diet down to a lower classification because the team's best wrestler or an inter- scholastic champion happens to be in his "normal" class. Not only is this likely to be poor judgment from a physical standpoint—that is, he's liable to be weakening himself—but it's not very good psychologically either. A boy has to be positive in order to be successful.

Regardless of a boy's size, he should never have to struggle to keep within his weight class. If, before a tournament, he skips meals, or runs or exercises strenuously while wearing a rubber suit in order to make weight, then he is undoubtedly in the wrong class. He should always be at peak strength when a tournament nears, and he can't be if he is crash-dieting or overexercising.

COMPETITION

Youngsters usually first become exposed to wrestling at summer camp, in grade school or high school. It is also becoming increasingly popular as a college sport, and in parts of Iowa, Oklahoma and Califor- nia, wrestling matches can outdraw basketball games.

The AAU has done a great deal to expand wrestling competition in recent years, developing a program patterned after its successful swimming and track programs. The organization's goal is to develop 1,000 wrestling clubs and register 50,000 amateur wrestlers between the ages of five and twenty-five.

As part of its ambitious plan, the AAU sponsored the first National Junior Olympic Wrestling Championships in 1970, the first National Junior Greco-Roman Championships in 1971, and, the same year, the first National Age-Group Tournament for both Greco-Roman and freestyle. (Freestyle wrestling permits the application of legal holds to all parts of the body. In Greco-Roman, holds are restricted to the upper body; the use of the legs is excluded.) Twelve national wrestling cham- pionships were contested in 1973 under the auspices of the AAU.

Wrestling also offers youngsters a chance for international com- petition. Each year junior (and senior) teams are selected to represent the United States in championship matches sponsored by the Interna- tional Amateur Wrestling Foundation.

A wrestling match involves two boys of approximately the same weight who compete on foam-rubber mats, which have been so marked that the wrestling area takes the form of a circle 28 feet in diameter or a 28-foot square. High school matches are six minutes in length

Wrestling

and divided into three two-minute periods, but there is no rest-time between periods.

A referee controls the match, watching for illegal or dangerous holds. He also awards all the points. The object of the match is for one man to defeat the other by means of a fall (also called a pin), which is scored by throwing or forcing one's opponent down on his shoulders, and holding him there for a two-second count (one second in college competition). The referee slams his hand on the mat to indicate a fall, which ends the match.

If neither man scores a fall, the bout is decided by points. A takedown is worth 2 points; an escape, 1 point; a reversal, 2 points; a predicament, 2 points; and a near fall, 3 points. When a rule is violated, penalty points are handed out, usually 1 point for each infraction. The referee signals the scorekeeper when awarding a point or penalizing a wrestler.

In dual meets, competition begins with the lightest-weight contestants and progresses to the heavyweights. Team points are scored as follows: victory by a fall, 5 points; victory by a decision, 3 points; match ending in a draw, 2 points for each team. Forfeits and defaults are scored as falls.

Wrestlers wear either tight-fitting shorts or full-length jersey tights. The body must be covered below the armpits. Ear guards are mandatory. Some wrestlers wear lightweight knee pads, but these are optional. Wrestling footwear consists of flat-soled canvas or leather shoes laced so as to cover the ankle.

BOOKS AND PUBLICATIONS

The AAU (3400 West 86th St., Indianapolis, Ind. 46268) will, upon request, send you a comprehensive wrestling bibliography, listing books, magazines, newspapers and films. The organization's *Official Wrestling Handbook,* a complete and up-to-date review of the sport, is especially valuable.

For a rundown of the rules of wrestling followed in college competition, obtain a copy of *Wrestling Guide,* published by the College Athletics Publishing Service (349 East Thomas Road, Phoenix, Ariz. 85000). It costs $1.50.

Inside Wrestling (Henry Regnery Co., $1.95), by Tom Valentine, explains wrestling's holds and counters. The reader benefits from scores of line drawings and photographs. It's a relatively new book, published in 1972. The author is wrestling coach at Northwestern University.

BOXING

Amateur boxing seldom gains public attention, except when it happens to produce a George Foreman or Muhammad Ali. Yet schools, colleges and youth organizations such as the Boys' Clubs of America continue to support boxing competition, and each year the Golden Gloves attracts tens of thousands of eager competitors.

The Police Athletic League (PAL) sponsors boxing programs in New York, Philadelphia, San Francisco and many other large cities. So does the YMCA and the Catholic Youth Organization (CYO). In Chicago, the Mayor Daley Foundation is active in boxing promotion.

Most amateur boxing programs follow the weight divisions established by the AAU: 112 pounds, 118, 125, 135, 139, 147, 158, 168, 175, and heavyweight. There are no draws in amateur boxing. The officials—usually two judges and a referee—must render a decision.

Bouts consist of three two-minute rounds. Interscholastic rules recommend 10-ounce gloves for all weight classes up to and including featherweight (125 pounds) and 12 ounces in all other classes.

Amateur boxers wear headguards in both training *and* competition. These provide a thick layer of kapok or foam rubber to protect the head, ears and cheekbones. When of proper fit, the headpiece should just cover the wearer's eyebrows. A mouthpiece is another vital

piece of equipment. Coaches want their boxers to use a fitted mouth-piece, one manufactured by the wearer's family dentist. The white rubber mouthpiece sold in sporting goods stores doesn't give adequate protection.

Handwraps, long strips of cotton cloth with thumb straps and tie strings, are also important. These serve to keep the knuckles depressed into the back of the hand so that they will be on the same plane as the wrist when a blow is struck. They should be worn anytime the boxer puts on a pair of gloves, even for a training session with the light bag.

Young boxers are taught three principal types of punches: straight-arm punches, such as the straight right and left jab; hooks, bent-arm blows directed to the body or head; and uppercuts, short blows directed upward, frequently to the opponent's chin.

Defensive skills include blocking, stopping blows with one's arms, elbows, shoulders or hands; parrying, deflecting an opponent's blow with one's gloves or forearms; slipping, moving the head or body to either side to avoid a lead or counter; and ducking, which needs no defining.

For information regarding boxing instruction, contact the local chapter of any one of the organizations mentioned in the opening paragraphs of this section. Very few books are available containing boxing instruction. But one is *Better Boxing for Boys* (Dodd, Mead & Co., $3.50), which I wrote several years ago in cooperation with the Director of Boxing of the Department of Parks and Recreation of the City of New York.

JUDO
AND
KARATE

Some definitions first.

Judo is a specialized form of unarmed self-defense involving a multiplicity of falls, holds and throws.

Karate is a system of unarmed self-defense which involves the use of the hands, elbows, knees or feet for kicks and blows to vulnerable parts of the body, such as the temple, throat or groin. There is no grasping or grappling.

While both of these have obvious limitations as to their physiological benefits, each has value in helping to improve a youngster's muscle tone and coordination. Of course, the benefits that are to be derived are closely linked to the amount and frequency of training sessions.

Be aware that training and instruction in judo as a sport have little to do with preparing a person to engage in a street brawl or to fend off a mugger. In sport judo, the partners bow, grasp each other in carefully prescribed fashion, and then attempt to maneuver each other into an off-balance position for throwing.

The same with karate; sport karate is different from karate for self-defense. Each involves a different set of skills. For example, in sport karate, only the high kicks are allowed, and kicks below the waist have no point value. But in using karate for self-defense, the low kicks can be telling blows.

GETTING INSTRUCTION

Judo and karate schools are everywhere. There are likely to be several pages of listings and advertisements in the Yellow Pages of your telephone directory (under the heading "Judo, Karate & Jiu-Jitsu Instruction"), particularly if you live in an urban area. YMCAs and school adult education departments also offer courses, as do many elementary and high schools.

When planning to deal with a commercial school, one that charges for lessons on a contractual basis, do as much investigation as you can in advance. Observe a junior class in session and establish that the students are actually being taught. No reliable school will refuse your request to be a guest during an instruction period.

Some instructors merely demonstrate a particular technique and then tell their students to imitate it as best they can. A real teacher will explain each fundamental, demonstrate it, then, as the students imitate the demonstration, he will constructively criticize and correct each one. Once the student can perform the exercise, he should be instructed to keep repeating it until he can do it instinctively. The class itself should be small enough so that individual attention is no problem. Of course, the instructor's attitude is important, too; he should be patient, understanding and enthusiastic.

Don't be misled by the fact that the instructor happens to wear a black belt or is qualified to wear one. The black belt is evidence that he is a skilled performer, but gives no indication of his ability as a teacher.

Also appraise the school as to cleanliness and safety. Mats for judo practice should be thick enough to take the sting out of falls. The practice of contact blows should be performed in slow motion. Defensive hitting should be accomplished by light, just-touching blows. Any hard hitting should be practiced against the training bag.

Once you are satisfied on these matters, discuss the contract terms in detail. Almost all schools specify a certain fee for a given number of lessons. Since you have no way of gauging whether your son or daughter will maintain interest in the course to the very end, it's wise to establish a per-lesson payment plan, rather than agree to pay a substantial portion of the tuition in advance and guarantee payment of the balance. Most schools will want a portion of the tuition in advance, and it is fair for them to ask for it. But don't pay the full amount in advance nor make a promise to pay the full amount unless your youngster attends every session.

Judo & Karate

Be wary of any school that charges more than $100 for a series of group lessons, promises a rank upon completion of the course, or applies pressure tactics, the type sometimes associated with the health-club field.

The AAU and the USJF (the United States Judo Foundation) have "recognized" hundreds of judo clubs, and dealing with one of these gives you some assurance that you will be dealing with qualified and ethical personnel. Contact the local chapter of either one of these organizations and ask to consult the list of recognized clubs. Many clubs are listed in the *Official Judo Handbook* published by these organizations (see below).

Schools often sell the traditional costume for judo, which consists of double-woven cotton trousers reaching to just below the knees, and a loose jacket of the same material with sleeves reaching to just below the elbows. A cloth belt, which goes twice around the jacket at the waist, completes the outfit. The suits cost about $10.

Bear in mind that suits are usually not preshrunk, so order a size that is overly large. The suit for karate is similar but made of lighter-weight material.

JUNIOR COMPETITION

Judo competition in the United States is sponsored jointly by the AAU (3400 West 86th St., Indianapolis, Ind. 46268) and the USJF (4367 Bishop Rd., Detroit, Mich. 48224). The AAU sanctions contests and certifies the amateur standing of contestants, while the USJF, an organization composed of twenty-three regional Black Belt associations, trains and examines instructors and officials, certifies candidates for promotion from one competitive level to the next, and oversees other such technical matters.

The AAU and USJF established a Junior Division in 1964 and have been actively promoting the sport since that time. There are eight age-weight divisions (beginning at age nine and 68 pounds) and both a lightweight and heavyweight category within each division. No junior competitor can be older than sixteen.

Contests are usually fifteen minutes in length. Points are awarded under any of the following conditions: a contestant is thrown to the mat with appreciable force; a contestant is held on his back under control for thirty seconds; a contestant is choked into submission; a contestant is forced to surrender because a joint, usually the elbow, is in danger of being broken.

Karate does not lend itself to competition as well as judo. Tournament contestants engage in sparring matches in which attacks and defenses are simulated. The kicks and blows are halted just short of contact, or they are delivered with controlled contact. Judges decide whether the attacks could have been effective and points are awarded accordingly. The United States Karate Foundation (135 West 23rd St., New York, N.Y. 10011) has established the rules and regulations governing championship competition.

INSTRUCTION BOOKS

The AAU (see address above) has compiled extensive bibliographies on both judo and karate. Write and request them. If competitive judo is your child's particular interest, don't fail to obtain a copy of the *Official Judo Handbook,* a joint publication of the AAU and USJF.

Then there are the books of Bruce Tegner. Tegner is without a doubt the best-known American instructor of the Oriental fighting arts. From California and the son of parents who were both black-belt holders and professional instructors, Tegner began to receive instruction at the age of two. Throughout his childhood, he was taught by high-

Judo & Karate

ranking Oriental and European masters, and at fifteen he began his career as a professional instructor. He operates his own school in Hollywood, where he has taught thousands. He has also taught instructors of weaponless combat in the U.S. Marine Corps and served as a consultant to law enforcement agencies and college police science departments.

Tegner has written about thirty paperback books on judo and karate, examining these sports from every aspect, and most titles are easily available. If your youngster is enrolled in an instruction course, buy him a book that covers the topics the course is to cover. By reading the text and checking the photos, he'll be able to review the subject matter discussed and get an idea of what is to come as well. The book will also be helpful to him in setting up solo practice sessions.

VII   TEAM SPORTS

BASEBALL
FOOTBALL
BASKETBALL
SOCCER
SOFTBALL
ICE HOCKEY
VOLLEYBALL
GYMNASTICS
TRACK AND FIELD

TEAM SPORTS
IN GENERAL

Team sports in America are a mixed blessing, which is one of the few general statements that you can make about them. Much depends on which sport you're talking about (for example, baseball's values are modest when compared to those of basketball), the age of the participant, and the program itself—that is, how it is directed and supervised. This last is particularly important.

Team sports, when compared to individual sports such as ice skating or golf, offer one benefit that must be mentioned at once, however. They provide the child with the simple pleasure of being with other children. Running, jumping, yelling, shouting, shoving and being shoved—don't underestimate the value of these.

Competitive team sports are offered by a wide variety of organizations, by schools and park departments, by YMCAs and large numbers of private organizations like the Little Leagues. No matter what the sport or the sponsoring organization, there are certain guidelines to look for. Safety is foremost. Be certain the team is going to use safety equipment. If it's baseball, there should be batters' helmets, catching gear, and all the rest. If it's football, there should be the array of padded and cushioned gear needed for that sport. The practice field and playing field should be such that they are not going to contribute to injury.

If your child is provided with quality equipment and is well supervised, the chances of his being injured are few. Indeed, serious injuries are unusual in team sports and broken bones are rare. The injuries that do occur are scrapes and bruises, the same type he might sustain while playing in the backyard.

Before your child joins a team or embarks on a new sport, take him to the family doctor for a physical examination. Explain to the doctor the type of sport the child is going to be playing. Chronic conditions for which the child may be undergoing treatment—hay fever, diabetes, even epilepsy—don't necessarily rule out organized team sports. The decision as to whether a youngster can or cannot participate has to be based on the particular case, on the severity of the condition as related to the sport involved.

Should your youngster sustain a minor injury during a game, he should be immediately removed and not permitted to return to the game until he has completely recovered. Youngsters watch pro football on television and see heavily bandaged, limping and sometimes bleeding players taking part in games, and they hear these men being praised for being so valiant. It's no wonder that millions of American youngsters think that there's something noble about "playing hurt." This attitude must be discouraged. A youngster who takes part in a game after having suffered a minor injury is risking serious injury.

A word about drugs as they apply to injured players. Don't limit your concept of what drugs are to the sophisticated painkillers or well-publicized stimulants, the so-called "greenies" that Jim Bouton spoke of. Think of drugs in a much broader sense. According to the dictionary, a drug is "a substance used as medicine in the treatment of a disease or other ailment." That's how to think of drugs, as any "substance used in treatment." Aspirin is a drug and so is rubbing alcohol. Each has its place, but each should be used with discretion. "It should be emphasized that drugs—even aspirin—should not be used to keep a child on his feet for a game," says Dr. Merritt B. Low, a well-known authority on sports and young athletes. "Even local drugs (such as a liniment) and bandaging should not be used (as they are in the 'pros') just to get an injured child through a given episode or important contest."

The matter of safety also includes the quality of supervision—*adult* supervision—the youngster is to receive. The coaches should be knowledgeable and experienced. Games should be conducted with a respect for the rules, with officials provided. In case of contact sports, there should be medical supervision.

There's an emotional aspect of competitive sports that must be weighed, too. In recent years countless psychiatrists and psychologists have spoken out in opposition to competitive sports for the pre-adolescent child. Not only may a sport be harmful in itself, but the problem is worsened by the schools that place too much of an emphasis on varsity sports. It results in the glorification of a handful of athletes, a kind of a star system. For a boy who is deeply interested in sports but limited as to ability, this situation inevitably leads to his "not making the team," to failure. He may react by becoming a spectator—for the rest of his life.

This is why it is best if the teams in a given league be formed on the basis of the size of the players, their height and weight, not on the basis of age. But this seldom holds true. Adults have been grouping youngsters by chronological age or school grades for generations because it's simple and saves time, and it's not likely that the policy is going to end very soon. But there should be some consideration given to the matter of physical maturity when teams are being formed.

If your youngster is slow in developing, he may spend most of his time on the sidelines, even though he has finely honed skills. It's just that his size, or lack of it, is too much of a disadvantage. For this reason, it would be well for junior leagues to institute a rule that grants a minimum amount of playing time to each youngster. Suppose your youngster is on a baseball team; he attends all the practice sessions, pays whatever fees are involved, and provides the necessary equipment. If the team plays fourteen games, each seven innings, your youngster should play twenty innings, or something more or less than that. A similar policy should exist in basketball or football—any team sport. No coach or supervisor can really find fault with this plan.

More and more, the matter of winning vs. losing is becoming a problem in team sports for youngsters. Vince Lombardi's maxim that "winning isn't everything, it's the only thing" has sifted down to high school and the Little Leagues. Winning may have been the "only thing" for the Green Bay Packers of the 1960s and present-day professional football teams, but it shouldn't be any young person's guiding principle, for with it goes the ruthlessness, brutality and high injury rate that often characterize the pro game.

This is not to say that winning isn't important. No sport, no game, whether it be lawn tennis or Chinese checkers, can have any meaning unless the opposing sides make a determined effort to trim one another. *A determined effort*—that's what to expect from your child. You want him to do his level best.

Sure, he's going to be sad when his team loses and happy when it wins. You want that, too. But he should be able to cope with either.

One parent I know whose son has participated in high school basketball for three years now, and grammar school sports before that, classifies coaches as being of one of two kinds. The type he looks for are teachers that coach. With this type he knows that his youngster is going to learn, going to enjoy. But with the other type, men who are coaches first and teachers only incidentally, he's wary. This type, he knows, can put too much stress on winning.

Get to know your son's coach, know his coaching philosophy. A good coach will welcome your interest. He realizes that the better he knows the parents of a player, the greater will be his understanding of the boy.

Your son's coach should be a leader, not merely a person with authority. He should have a profound knowledge of the sport and be skilled in teaching it, but he also must be capable of guiding youngsters in all other respects. Your son will probably spend more time with his coach than with any of the other teachers, and thus will probably be more influenced by him than any of the others.

The coach has to be firm and forceful, but also patient, understanding and considerate of young people and their needs and feelings. He has to be enthusiastic; he has to have self-control.

Do sports—organized high school team sports—help a youngster's studies? Probably. A study conducted by a pair of sociologists from the University of Oregon found that the more a high school athlete participated in sports, the higher were his grades in comparison to those of nonathletes, although just why they were higher wasn't clearly established.

The study covered 585 boys representing two Midwestern high schools; 164 of the boys were athletes. The students were graded for three years on a numerical scale (A equaled 4, B equaled 3, C equaled 2, D equaled 1, and F equaled 0). Grades of athletes averaged out to 2.35 or C, while those of nonathletes were 1.83 or D. When 304 athletes and nonathletes of similar IQs were compared, the athletes did slightly better, 2.35 to 2.24.

The study found that athletes in minor sports (what the professors

Team Sports in General

defined as all sports but football and basketball) received better grades than those in major sports. However, the football and basketball players were academically much further ahead of nonathletes with comparable IQs than the players of minor sports.

The professors offered a list of possible explanations as to why the athletes did better. It may have been, they said, that the athletes were graded more leniently, or that the discipline of sports led the athletes to make better use of their study time, or that the prestige of athletics led to increased confidence.

The study indicated that more athletes than nonathletes expected to go to college, and that almost five times as many nonathletes dropped out of high school. The authors concluded that athletics exerts a "holding influence" on students tempted to quit school.

One other area of sports instruction and participation for children must be mentioned. It's the sports camp. I'm referring to the private camps, usually located in the mountain, lake or seashore regions of the country, which offer concentrated instruction in a particular sport. You can enroll a youngster for a full summer of eight weeks, or sometimes a four-week program is offered. Football, basketball, baseball and individual sports such as tennis, skiing, riding and golf are some of those in which these camps specialize.

In selecting a camp for your youngster, speak to the parents of campers and obtain booklets and brochures from as many camps as you can. Study each one carefully, then make plans to visit the two or three camps that seem most appealing. Many camps schedule an "open house" for parents in advance of the camping season. If you plan far enough ahead, you can visit a camp during the season with the idea that your youngster may be attending the camp the following year. If a camp director is not enthusiastic about having you visit, be cautious. Ask the director to show you references from the parents of campers.

When you do visit a camp, inspect the facilities carefully and ask questions freely. The camp buildings should be clean, safe and in good repair. The dining room and kitchen should be screened. Modern refrigeration is a hallmark of a good camp.

The sleeping quarters should be roomy and well ventilated. No more than eight campers and one counselor should be assigned to a room. There should be adequate and easily accessible showers and toilets.

Be sure that the camp has a doctor and dentist on call at all times.

A registered nurse on the premises will ensure immediate treatment in case of injury or illness.

In many areas of the country, state health departments inspect camp sanitary facilities and water-supply systems. They also survey the source of camp milk supply, inspect screening and refrigeration, and examine safety conditions. They then rate or license the camps on the basis of their findings. Ask about such ratings or certificates of compliance when you visit the camp.

If the camp is located a good distance from where you live and a visit isn't convenient, try to talk to parents of children who have been campers. Or your child may know a youngster who is knowledgeable about the camp. These reports can be extremely valuable.

Some camps cite membership in the American Camping Association, an organization of camps, camp owners and directors, as being evidence of their excellence. The ACA requires certain minimum standards for accreditation; however, membership alone is not necessarily an indication of a camp's merit. You have to take the time to inspect the camp yourself.

It can cost as much as $1,300 or $1,400 to send a child to a sports camp for a full eight-week period. For children enrolled for half a season, four weeks, the charge is slightly more than half the full amount. At some camps, the tuition charge covers just about everything, while at others there are extra charges for insurance, laundry, day trips, transportation (to and from the bus depot or railroad station), and equipment extras like tennis balls, golf balls, football chin straps, etc.

Even though the camp features a specialty, it should offer a variety of other interests, allowing campers to make individual choices. Ask the director to show you a camp schedule for a particular day.

It's important to appraise the camp on the basis of instructors and counselors. There should be a ratio of one counselor for every eight or nine campers.

Don't allow yourself to be misled—as the child is likely to be—by the fact that a celebrity athlete owns the camp, endorses it, or has promised to be on hand during the weeks of instruction. Youngsters do like to meet a Willis Reed or a Joe Namath. It's a thrill for a boy to be on the same playing field with professionals of this stature, and maybe to have the star athlete say "Try holding the ball like this," or simply "Nice going." But pro superstars seldom have the time or inclination to give a youngster the type of instruction he requires. Instruction is an art. It takes patience; it takes the ability to enjoy teaching the youngster who may not be particularly skilled as an athlete.

220

Team Sports in General

What your youngster does need is someone who not only knows the sport in which the boy is interested, but is the sort of person he can relate to during the weeks of his camping stay. Many camps do have instructors of this type. They're coaches from prep schools or high schools, or quite often they're college athletes. Your child will learn from them; just as important, he'll find them enjoyable companions. And the child's enjoyment, after all, should be the leading objective of any sports program in which he becomes involved.

BASEBALL

Some people say that professional football is threatening baseball's status as "our national pastime." Maybe; but when it comes to junior competition, baseball is still several jumps ahead.

Baseball is played by thousands of high school teams and countless amateur and semiprofessional teams, categories which include the vast American Legion Junior Baseball program. There is Babe Ruth Baseball and Boys Baseball, Inc., and, in most suburban areas, there are more Little Leagues than supermarkets. No one knows for certain how many youngsters are involved in junior baseball, but the number is well up in the millions.

Be sure to evaluate the safety aspects of any program in which your son participates, not only as far as game conditions are concerned, but also in tryouts and practice sessions. First-aid equipment should be available at the field, and there should be arrangements for emergency medical services. In Little League baseball, each league has a Safety Officer whose responsibility it is to provide safe practice and playing conditions.

Batters should wear helmets when they come up to the plate, and they should fit properly. The same with catcher's equipment; if it's too small or too big it doesn't give adequate protection.

Baseball

Chain-link fencing should protect dugouts, bat racks and on-deck areas. The playing area should be well maintained. Someone should be responsible for keeping bats and other pieces of equipment off the field of play. During a practice session or a game, only players, managers, coaches and umpires should be permitted on the field.

The physical trappings are only one aspect of it. The fact that your son becomes a member of a baseball team, Little League or otherwise, is no guarantee that he is going to be involved in a wholesome, enriching experience. Indeed, it can even be detrimental.

Sometimes there is an overemphasis on winning, a glorification of the best players and best teams. Players are allowed to become less than gracious in defeat. Opponents and officials come to be treated discourteously.

The standards of team conduct are set by the manager, a person you should regard as being crucial to what your child derives from baseball. How was the manager selected? On what basis? What type of person is he? It requires four years of college training to become a school physical-education instructor, but an individual can become the manager of a boys' baseball team simply because he knows how to fill out a line-up card and happens to have the time available. Investigate. Be sure your son is getting intelligent leadership.

When a program is harmful to a youngster, it is not always the fault of the manager or the league officials. Sometimes parents are to blame. They badger coaches, argue with umpires and berate their offspring. They *demand* victory. Children want the support of their parents, and they like to have them in the stands for a game. But exaggerated enthusiasm embarrasses them.

EQUIPMENT

There's probably not a great deal you can tell your son about baseball equipment. He is almost sure to know what he wants in the way of a glove and bat, and he can probably tell you the best place to buy it.

Bats for young players range in length from 27 inches to 32 inches. They are also now available in several different materials. There is the traditional wood bat, of course, and there are also aluminum and magnesium bats. The metal bat has the advantage that it won't crack, and although the initial cost is three· or four times that of the wood you never have to pay for a replacement. Like wood bats, metal bats are available in several lengths and weights.

Recently, AMF Voit introduced a nylon bat. It looks like wood and sounds like wood, but it's just as durable (and costs about the same) as the metal bat. About the only perceivable difference is a thin strip of color near the bat end that tells its weight and length—orange is 27 inches, yellow is 28 inches, etc. Nylon, aluminum and magnesium bats have all been approved for Little League play.

Fielder's gloves have gone mod and are available in brilliant blues and scarlet reds. Buy a glove that gives your youngster a snug, confident fit. An adjustable wrist strap helps. More expensive gloves have been pre-softened and pre-molded so that no breaking-in period is required.

JUNIOR LEAGUES

For almost forty years, under a system of volunteer participation and supervision, Little League baseball has shown consistent growth, taking root in just about every community. "Build a Better Boy" is the

Baseball

theme that the Little League program has adopted. Whether it always accomplishes this goal is the subject of constant debate. Nevertheless, the stability of the program is beyond doubt.

Little League baseball has two structural components—the administrative headquarters in Williamsport, Pennsylvania, and its local leagues, of which there are more than 6,000. Leagues can be organized in any neighborhood or community with a population of 15,000. League organizers make arrangements to procure a playing area and team sponsors, arrange for team managers and game umpires, purchase equipment and uniforms, and obtain financial support. Once a charter has been granted, the league operates autonomously, but it must adhere to regulations established by Little League Baseball, Inc., in Williamsport. The basic structural makeup of the program is explained in detail in literature available from Little League headquarters (P.O. Box 1127, Williamsport, Penna. 17701).

Any boy who has not reached his thirteenth birthday before August 1 of the current year (and lives within the geographical boundaries established in the league charter) is eligible for Little League competition. In 1961, Little League baseball introduced its Senior Division for boys thirteen to fifteen years old.

Eligible boys are brought together in the spring for a series of tryouts. Their ability to run, throw, field and hit is evaluated under the supervision of a parent known as a "player agent" and league managers and coaches. Player attitude is also appraised. "You want boys with the most hustle and desire," says the Little League Training Handbook. On the basis of the tryouts, each candidate is given a point score. Often it is based on this scale:

```
Best runner......................................8 points
Best throw for distance ..........................5 points
Best throwing accuracy ...........................3 points
Batting skill and power...........................5 points
Bunting skill ....................................2 points
Fielding skill ...................................4 points
Attitude .........................................3 points
Maximum score.....................................30 points
```

Boys who fail to score sufficient points to win positions on a team are sometimes retained in the program by being assigned to a minor-league team. Competition is held on diamonds that are scaled down

225

226

Baseball

to two-thirds major-league size. With seniors, however, competition is held on standard-size fields.

The Babe Ruth baseball program, founded in 1952, originally provided competition for thirteen-to-fifteen-year-old boys, but in 1966 the program was expanded with the introduction of a division for sixteen-to-eighteen-year-olds. Both divisions play on regulation-size fields and use slightly modified baseball rules.

The Babe Ruth program is similar to Little League baseball in the way it is structured. More information on the program can be obtained from Babe Ruth League headquarters (P.O. Box 5000, 1770 Brunswick Ave., Trenton, N.J. 08638).

Boys Baseball, Inc. (P.O. Box 225, Washington, Penna. 15301), which dates to 1950, offers Mustang Leagues (for boys nine and ten), Bronco Leagues (boys eleven and twelve), Pony Leagues (boys thirteen and fourteen), and Colt Leagues (boys fifteen and sixteen). About 150,000 youngsters are active in the program.

SKILL DRILLS

The best way to help your youngster improve his hitting is to put up a batting range in the back yard. You need an area about 10 feet by 30 feet. You need a batting tee and a supply of plastic balls. String a net or a piece of canvas between two poles. Place the batting tee about 20 feet from it. Adjust the height of the tee so that the youngster will, with a proper swing, hit line drives. By watching the flight of the ball, he should be able to judge whether he is hitting straight away, to right or left field, or over or under the ball.

By erecting pitching "strings" you can enable him to improve his delivery and control. The first step is to make a home plate out of scrap wood; paint it white. Anchor it in the ground with wooden pegs.

A pair of wood poles, 10 feet apart and about 5 feet above ground level, should then be sunk into the ground on either side of the plate. The poles' forward plane should line up with the front edge of the plate. The final step is to string tape between the posts so that a rectangle is formed that approximates the strike zone in size. One horizontal length of tape should be at knee level to a batter of average size, the other at armpit level. Then string vertical lengths of tape between the two horizontal lengths. They should be as far apart as the width of the plate. Use tape that is about ⅛ inch wide and strong enough to withstand being struck by the ball.

You can build a practice pitching mound and, at a distance of 44 feet from the strings, anchor a pitching slab made from scrap wood. Use wooden pegs to hold the slab in place.

The only other practice facility you'll need is a sliding pit. This requires an area about 6 feet by 12 feet. Dig it out to a depth of about 18 inches and fill it with fine sand.

FOOTBALL

"Football is two things, blocking and tackling," said Vince Lombardi. "I don't care anything about fancy formations or new stunts on defense. If you block and tackle better than the other team, you'll win."

This does, indeed, describe the basic elements of the game. Football is contact; football is hitting hard.

Naturally, injuries occur. But there is much you can do to help prevent them.

Be certain your youngster is not involved in a program in which he is going to be significantly outweighed by opposition players. The Pop Warner Junior League Football program (see below) boasts an admirable safety record, and a principal reason is that the organization permits competition only between youngsters of the same relative size through a system of age-weight classifications. In many grade school and high school programs, no such concept exists.

Occasionally injuries result because a boy is overly aggressive—that is, too aggressive in relation to his ability. He overextends himself; he places himself in situations with which he cannot physically cope.

Still another type of athlete is aggressive to such a degree that he feels cloaked with invulnerability. He thrives upon the contact, the collision of bodies, that is so much a part of football, and he may take unnecessary risks to demonstrate his omnipotence.

At the other extreme is the boy who fears injury. He puts out an arm to cushion a fall or cringes when he is about to be blocked or tackled. He shouldn't be playing football.

Coaches tell of boys who fail to report injuries for fear of being removed from the game. The concealment of minor injuries can lead to more serious ones. And then there are the coaches who permit injured youngsters to play, an idiocy covered in the introduction to this section, "Team Sports in General."

Of course, proper equipment is vital. It should meet these standards:

Helmet. There are two basic types of helmets, sponge-padded and suspension. The suspension type is usually recommended for young players. It consists of a framework of rugged straps that encircle the head, so that it never comes in contact with the helmet shell.

The helmet is just about worthless unless it fits properly. The Rawlings Company (2300 Delmar Blvd., St. Louis, Mo. 63166) has prepared a helmet-sizing guide which can be consulted to help get the right fit. Write for a copy or ask your sporting goods dealer whether he has one. The helmet fit should be on the snug side; there should be no slippage. The front edge should come no lower than ¼ inch above the eyebrows. Another test for fit is to see if the helmet earholes are centered over the openings of the ears. During the season, check the helmet's fit from time to time.

The helmet should be equipped with a facemask, the style depending on the player's position. Linemen wear what is called a "bird cage," a type with three horizontal bars and a vertical center bar. It gives complete protection to the face. Defensive backs, who require unobstructed vision at all times, wear a mask with only two horizontal bars.

Teeth protector. Get your youngster a custom-fitted mouthpiece. Consult your family dentist. Be sure he wears it for practice sessions as well as during games.

Shoulder pads. Here, as in the case of the helmet, careful attention should be given to fit. Rawlings has prepared a shoulder-pad "computer" to aid in getting the right size. Be sure the neck opening is large enough so that the wearer can, after donning his jersey, raise his arms over his head without the pads pinching his neck.

As for materials and construction, the pads should be made of

230

molded fiber or high-density polyethylene, and should have polyvinyl washable padding, heavy-duty web hinges and underarm straps. Be sure the upper wings absorb the shock of a blow and do not transmit it to the shoulder itself.

Hip and kidney pads.   Most professional players shun the use of hip pads, but young players should wear them. They should be made of molded fiber or polyethylene and backed with shock-absorbing foam rubber.

Thigh, knee and shin pads.   These, too, should consist of a durable outer surface backed by foam rubber. They are usually inserted into special pockets built into the football pants.

Pants.   While pants should be snug-fitting, they must be large enough to accommodate thigh pads and still give freedom of movement. Some pants feature snap-in hip and kidney pads. Every player should wear an athletic supporter. A plastic cup is considered optional.

Footwear.   Boys of eight to twelve usually wear sneakers or soccer-style rubber-cleated shoes. Shoes with detachable cleats are worn by older youngsters.

POP WARNER FOOTBALL

Pop Warner Junior League Football, named for coaching's innovative Glenn Scobie (Pop) Warner, is the only national organization active in the promotion of junior football. Approximately 175,000 boys participate in the program, and about 50,000 adults as coaches, fund raisers and administrative personnel.

The basic unit in the administration of the program is the association, which consists of a group of adults who sponsor one or more teams, recruiting players from within prescribed boundaries. Four to ten teams constitute a league. Teams and leagues are usually sponsored by civic clubs, service clubs, fraternal groups or other community-oriented organizations.

Boys from eight through fifteen are eligible for participation in the program. These are the age and weight divisions:

Division	Ages	Weight (at registration)
Tiny Tot	8–10	40–65
Junior Peewee	8–10	50–75
Peewee	10–12	65–95
Junior Midget	10–12	80–110
Midget	11–13	90–120
Junior Bantam	12–14	105–135
Bantam	13–15	120–150

Games are played under the rules of the National Federation of State High School Athletic Associations or the NCAA, but there are variations in the size of the ball and the playing field; they are smaller for younger boys. Tiny Tots play seven-minute quarters; Junior Peewees and Peewees, eight-minute quarters.

Championships are decided on the basis of league won-lost records. To determine national champions, local records are interpreted by means of an evaluation formula which gives equal weight to a team's won-lost record and the scholastic standings of the members of the various teams. This is in contrast to the Little League's extensive post-season championship playoff program, which Pop

Football

Warner officials criticize as being detrimental to young players and their schoolwork.

Of course, the Pop Warner program has its critics, too, some of whom say that the program exerts excessive pressure on the immature. Officials of the organization reply that it is the parents and coaches who must bear the responsibility for this. "Coaches who display the Vince Lombardi attitude," says David G. Tomlin, Pop Warner Vice President, "are quickly weeded out of local programs."

More information about Pop Warner Little League Football, including a handbook of the organization's basic rules and regulations, can be obtained by writing to the organization. Its address: 1041 Western Savings Bank Building, Philadelphia, Penna. 19107.

OTHER FOOTBALL GAMES

There are many variations of so-called tackle football, and all are well-suited for young players. Touch football is the best known. A play is ended when the ball carrier is touched by a defending player. It can be one hand or two; it depends upon the ground rules.

Teams can be of any size, and so can the field. In most versions of the game, the ball must be passed or kicked on every play.

Flag football is growing in popularity. The standard rules of football apply and the basic skills of the game are featured, except that there is no tackling. Ball carriers and pass receivers wear a small flag in a special waist belt. Snatching away a man's flag is the same as tackling him. Additional information on the game can be obtained from Pop Warner headquarters (see address above).

Two exciting versions of standard eleven-man tackle football are six-man football and eight-man football. Each is played on a field that is 80 yards long and 40 yards wide.

A six-man team consists of three linemen and three backfield men. An eight-man team has five linemen and three backs. In each game the pass is mandatory; there's no rushing the ball.

BASKETBALL

Basketball enjoys immense popularity, with an estimated 20,000 high schools fielding teams. But that is only the tip of the iceberg. City playgrounds offer basketball and little else, and the back yards and driveways of suburban America are well sprinkled with makeshift courts.

The rules of basketball state that the baskets are to be attached to the backboards "at a point 10 feet above the court surface." But the rules say nothing about the tallness of the players. This means that a man who happens to be tall has a big advantage: When he shoots or rebounds he is closer to the basket. In no other sport is a physical anomaly so valuable.

Basketball is more physically demanding than any other team sport, with the possible exception of some of the track and field events. Every part of the body is involved and the game requires tremendous stamina. But good size is a virtual must. Unless your son is going to be a 6-footer, don't encourage him to pursue basketball beyond the grade school level, at least not on a varsity basis. Sometimes a relatively short player excels in the sport, but it doesn't happen very often.

A word about stamina. Watch a game; watch the players pound up and down the court. A baseball player can abuse training rules occasionally; a football player, a lineman, can let himself get out of condition—and several games can be played before anyone catches on. But if a basketball player is not at a fitness peak, it's noticeable before the first quarter is very old.

Despite the emphasis on tallness, basketball's appeal is universal. The basic skill required—to be able to put the ball up and have it swish through the hoop—is one that any boy can master. For real success, however, many other skills are required, including speed, coordination and the ability to think quickly under pressure.

Practicing helps a great deal. Through practice sessions, a player can improve his shooting, passing, ball-handling, dribbling and guarding.

Women's basketball has changed drastically in recent years. The rules used to specify that the court be divided into two zones, and players occupying zones could not leave them. But nowadays girls play under virtually the same rules as boys, with one exception, a "thirty-second rule." This states that a team must give up the ball to the opposition if it fails to attempt a shot within thirty seconds.

There are a number of books on basketball available. Two good ones are *Inside Basketball,* by Dick Barnett (Regnery, $2.95); and *Basketball,* by Earl Monroe and Wes Unfeld (Atheneum, $4.95).

EQUIPMENT

The regulation basketball, 29 to 30 inches in circumference, weighs between 20 and 22 ounces when fully inflated. When dropped from a height of 6 feet, it should rebound at least 49 inches.

Basketball shoes can be high or low, leather or canvas, depending on the player's preference. The soles should give plenty of traction. Other qualities to look for are sponge-rubber insoles and laces that reach to the toe area.

Many players wear two pairs of socks, a soft lightweight-cotton inner sock and a heavier woolen sock. Two pairs of socks help to prevent blisters. Elbow pads and knee pads are worn sometimes.

If your son wears eyeglasses, have him wear an eyeglass protector, a metal or plastic frame which fits over the glasses. It's held in place by an adjustable head strap. If he feels such a device is objectionable, have him at least wear a head strap, the type that attaches to the eyeglass frames and fits about the back of the head to hold the glasses in place.

Basketball

SHOOTING

The kinds of shots that players take today would dazzle players of the past. Not only do they range in type from fast-driving layups and quick tip-ins to graceful fallaways, but each type can be executed in countless different ways. It's the age of the acrobat.

Nevertheless, one shot is pre-eminent: the one-hand jump shot. The player jumps straight up and "pops" the ball basketward at the very top of his jump. What makes the one-hand jumper so difficult to block is that only the shooter knows when he's going up. The defenseman can only guess.

Beginners who attempt the shot often make the mistake of allowing the elbow of the shooting arm to drift to the left or right as they get set to release. The elbow has to be positioned directly below the shooting hand in order to get sufficient leverage and assure accuracy.

A player getting off a shot from the right side uses his left foot as the takeoff foot. The forearm snaps forward and downward; the wrist uncocks. The ball should be allowed to roll off the fingers in such a way that backspin is created. Then the player must follow through, so that his arm is fully extended at the finish.

Today's young players use the one-hand jumper when at close or medium range, and almost all shooting from the foul line is done with one hand.

SOCCER

Until fairly recent times, soccer in the United States was a game played chiefly by foreign-born students or by ethnic clubs in big cities, but seldom by American-born youngsters. But this is changing, and very rapidly.

A survey conducted by the Professional North American Soccer League in 1965 found that only about 800 high schools, mostly in the Northeast, had soccer teams. A similar survey taken five years later showed that the number had expanded to 2,800. Today the figure is above 3,000 and still climbing. The number of college teams went from 225 in 1965 to 680 in 1970. Even more striking growth has been observed in elementary schools, with more than 5,000 of them adding the sport in recent years. It is really only a matter of time until soccer begins to compete with baseball and football as the sport most favored by American youngsters.

The reasons for soccer's appeal are easy to perceive. The game is less expensive than any other team sport (all you really need are a ball and a flat, open field), it is easier to organize, and it provides better exercise and more fun. About all that it doesn't have is spectator appeal, at least if the spectators happen to be American. American sports fans have been educated to expect electrifying moments (as the home run provides in baseball or the long "bomb" in football) or high scores (as in basketball).

Participants, however, have no complaints. Young players get joy out of the fact that they run a full sixty minutes in each game. In football, thirteen or fourteen minutes of action is a lot. In a baseball game, a Little Leaguer averages one time at bat per game, and most of his time in the field is spent waiting for something to happen.

Kyle Rote, Jr., son of the football hero from Southern Methodist and the New York Giants, gave up a football scholarship at Oklahoma State to play soccer at the University of the South in Tennessee. "I still like football, but soccer is the greater game, the greater challenge to the athlete," Rote has said. Young players echo this claim. "Every man on the team is a quarterback" is a remark heard frequently.

While heading the ball (striking it with one's head) and tackling (a blocking or interfering tactic used to take the ball away from an opposing player) cause their share of bruises and bloody noses, serious injuries seldom happen. In Finneytown, Ohio, a heavily German community, the Kolping Society and the Schwaben Club have helped to organize a junior soccer program that involves more than 3,200 youngsters. During one recent three-year period, only two serious injuries occurred.

"This is a sport any parent can love," says the mother of two youngsters who take part in the Finneytown program. "In our Little League program, the score would be nineteen to nothing and the mothers would all start going home because their sons would go to bat only once in an hour. But here your son is running all the time. He's just as tired whether he wins or loses."

It helps to be fast. It helps to be aggressive. But one's size is not an important factor, and neither is one's sex. Programs for girls are now being established in many areas.

EQUIPMENT

"I can outfit a boy for twenty dollars a season," says Bill Clarke, head soccer coach at Cleveland State University. "Make it fifty dollars if we include warmup jackets and practice uniforms. You couldn't buy one football helmet for that."

The fact that so little specialized equipment is required is one of soccer's chief appeals. A ball is about the only essential. An English "World Cup" ball, made of thirty-two stretched prime-leather panels bonded to a rugged vinyl carcass, costs about $25. But a rubber-cov-

ered ball, nylon-wound and with the same paneled construction, is perfectly adequate for practice and informal play, and costs less than $10.

For footwear, sneakers are all right for beginners, but for competition a player needs cleated boots. Look for shoes that give padded protection to the bridge of the foot and offer a flat-surfaced striking area. Quality boots start at about $15 and range up to $30.

Young goaltenders sometimes perform better if made to wear a body pad, a protective tunic of quilted plastic. A body pad costs about $14. Goalie gloves are $5. Lightweight shin pads are $3.50 a pair.

LEARNING THE FUNDAMENTALS

Throw a ball to an American youngster and he'll try to catch it. Throw one to a European boy and he'll trap it with his chest, drop it to his feet and kick it back. I'm not talking about a soccer ball necessarily; it happens with any type of ball. American youngsters, when it comes to ball sports, are hand-oriented; with European boys it's the feet.

This is because European children are taught to kick not long after they've gotten out of the Pablum stage. "When my son was two or three," says English soccer coach George Kirby, "I showed him how to kick a small rubber ball, no bigger than a tennis ball. I taught him how to control it with his feet.

"Later, when he was five, I bought him a small leather ball, about the size of a big grapefruit. When he went to school in the morning, and in the afternoon on the way home, he'd kick the ball in front of him. Many of his classmates did the same. Naturally, it was easy for him to learn how to kick and control a soccer ball."

The basic soccer kick is the instep kick. It's unlike a punt in football in that the ball is not kicked from the hip, and it's unlike a placekick in that the toe plays almost no part.

In executing the instep kick, the kicker strides forward and plants his nonkicking foot just outside and in back of the ball, then swings the kicking leg forward from the knee, the toes pointed down and slightly inward. The leg straightens as it swings through, the instep making contact slightly below the center of the ball.

Beginners sometimes have difficulty keeping the ball low because they have a tendency to get the toe into the kick, not the instep. Getting closer to the ball as the kick is executed helps to overcome this. Another way is to have your youngster practice kicking in his stocking feet; he'll quickly learn not to use his toes.

While your youngster shouldn't have any real difficulty learning to execute the instep kick with his right foot, it may be a different story as far as the left foot is concerned. By practicing, however, he can become skilled.

While learning to kick the ball is important, learning to control it

243

is *more* important. A young player has to have the ability to move the ball at any speed and in any direction. Good players have "feel" in their feet.

Ball control can be learned in solo drills. Simply running with the ball at one's feet is helpful; stopping and starting every 25 yards and swerving to the right and left add to the drill's difficulty.

Some coaches place a row of six or seven 3-foot stakes in the ground about 6 feet apart, then time their players as they run in and out of the stakes, first in one direction, then in the other, without a ball. They then time them with a ball. The idea, of course, is to get the time of the second run to equal the time of the first, or at least get it as close to equaling it as possible.

Dribbling can also be practiced by having the young player move in a circular pattern, first clockwise, then counterclockwise. He can vary the drill by controlling the ball with the inside of his foot on one run, with the outside of his foot on the next.

A young player can practice kicking the ball by rebounding it off a wall or the side of a building. He should become as skilled in kicking with the left foot as he is with the right, and he should know how to kick a ball that's coming toward him, high or low.

His kicking drills should be related to the position that he plans to play. A boy who is a forward should work on dribbling and quick crossing kicks. A fullback has to learn to execute long clearing kicks.

Passing drills are important, too. A youngster can practice passing to a target on a wall, a marker on the field, or, better yet, a teammate. Both trapping and heading can be practiced solo or with a teammate. A boy can trap a ball off the wall or get a partner to throw it to him. To practice heading, he simply bounces the ball several times in succession from his forehead straight up in the air, or two boys can head the ball back and forth.

CHOOSING A POSITION

Soccer is a fast-moving, fluid game, with possession of the ball constantly shifting back and forth from one team to the other.

Nevertheless, there are certain qualities that typify each of the playing positions. Soccer is played with an eleven-man team: a goalkeeper, two fullbacks, three halfbacks and five forwards. The forwards, the outside men in particular, have to have good speed; indeed, they must be the fastest men on the team. Agility is almost equal in impor-

Soccer

tance. Forwards also have to be able to pass or shoot with both feet with equal skill.

The halfbacks are key figures. They have a defensive role to play when enemy forwards are on the attack, and they also have to act in support of their own offensive line. The halfbacks control and handle the ball more than any of the other players. As this implies, each has to be agile and strong, and have more than the usual amount of stamina.

The center halfback is often rated the most important man on the field. He has to be fast, yet sturdily built, a master ball handler, and since he often sets the team's offensive and defensive tactics, he needs leadership qualities as well.

Fullbacks have to be strong, strong enough to be successful tacklers, and with legs powerful enough to get good distance with their kicks. Seldom does a fullback have to dribble; instead, he must be skilled at getting rid of the ball quickly.

A goalkeeper has to have strong arms, shoulders and legs, and sure hands. Good height helps but is not a necessity. Small, agile boys sometimes make fine goalies. The goalkeeper also has to have the ability to concentrate, and this, particularly in the case of young players, is not always a simple task. When play is at the opposite end of the field for a long time, it is very easy for a boy to let his attention wander. What he should be doing instead is studying the playing characteristics of the opposing players, their moves and their shots. This helps him to anticipate what is going to happen.

The goalkeeper also has a part to play as a field general, similar to the role of a catcher in baseball. When play comes close, he shouts warnings and instructions to his teammates. Finally, the goalkeeper has to have more than the usual amount of courage, the ability to remain cool in the face of shots taken at point-blank range.

ORGANIZATIONS

Organized soccer in this country is supervised by the United States Soccer Football Association (350 Fifth Ave., Room 4010, New York, N.Y. 10001). The organization provides the standard rules of play, sanctions tournaments, and oversees the conduct of the game in schools and colleges.

The USSFA also maintains an active role in the promotion of the game among junior players. Information on developing and organizing a junior soccer program can be obtained from the USSFA's Youth Promotion Committee (79 West Monroe St., Chicago, Ill. 60603). Soccer competition in Canada is supervised by the Dominion of Canada Football Association.

SOFTBALL

There is scarcely a boy or girl who has not played softball at one time or another. Competition is largely informal (although the Amateur Softball Association sponsors a well-developed league program), a fact that statistics bears out. The ASA has 600,000 registered players, adults included, but the organization estimates that the game is played by 30,000,000 people annually.

Softball was first played in the 1880s and the first league was established in 1897. But the sport didn't begin to develop in an organized manner until 1933, the year that the Amateur Softball Association was founded. Leo Fischer, sports editor of the Chicago *American* at the time, was the driving force behind the founding of the ASA, and its first president.

Softball resembles baseball in many aspects, but there are some important differences, chiefly in the technique of pitching. All pitching must be underhand, with the arm parallel to the body at the time the ball is released. Despite the underhand delivery, pitchers are able to fire the ball at bullet speed; in fact, scientific tests have shown that a pitcher in softball can throw with greater velocity than a baseball pitcher. Yet the pitching distance in softball is less than that in baseball,

46 feet (and even less in junior play) compared to 60 feet 6 inches. Little wonder that it is possible for a pitcher to dominate a game.

During the 1960s, a slow-pitch version of softball became popular, and today about 70 percent of all games are played according to the slow-pitch rule. This specifies that the ball must be delivered ''with a perceptible arch of at least 3 feet after it leaves the pitcher's hand.'' Under this rule, strikeouts are rare; the batter is a hitter.

Softball

PLAYING THE GAME

The softball playing field is smaller than the baseball field; bases are 60 feet apart (in adult play) as compared to baseball's 90 feet. For boys and girls in the nine-to-twelve age group, the bases are 45 feet apart and the pitching distance is 35 feet. For all other juniors, the distance between bases is the standard 60 feet, but the pitching distance remains 35 feet.

There are differences in equipment, too. The bat is smaller, with a maximum length of 34 inches and a maximum diameter of 2⅛ inches. Aluminum bats are used frequently at every level of play. A game is only seven innings long. Stealing bases is permitted, but the runner cannot leave his base until the pitcher releases the ball.

The leather-covered ball is smooth-seamed, packed with kapok which has been tightly wound with yarn. It weighs not less than 6 nor more than 6¾ ounces, and in circumference is between 11⅞ inches and 12⅛ inches.

The rules of softball distinguish between gloves and mitts. Gloves are five-fingered, while mitts have a separate sheath only for the thumb. Mitts can be worn only by catchers and first basemen; all other players must wear gloves. The principal baseball-equipment manufacturers—Wilson, Spalding and Rawlings—also offer a complete line of softball gloves and mitts.

Because of the relative smallness of the playing area, softball puts an emphasis on quickness, and this is true whether a player is at bat or in the field.

In batting, an open, closed or square stance can be used, but the man has to have the ability to get the bat around fast. It's seldom a cat-and-mouse game as it can be in baseball. The batter can't wait for a particular pitch or make up his mind beforehand that he is going to hit to a certain field. He has to hit what is thrown. Of course, he has to refrain from hitting bad pitches, but when the ball comes in high or low within the strike zone, he has to be able to hit squarely and sharply, to punch the ball.

In playing the infield or outfield, alertness is the key. The player always has to be ready to react. Softball places far greater importance on knowing the strengths and weaknesses of hitters, and adjusting one's position accordingly.

Quickness is also vital in baserunning. Since the rules specify that the baserunner cannot leave the base until the ball is pitched, he has to break at exactly the right instant. Being quick and perceptive is as important as having good speed afoot.

249

JUNIOR COMPETITION

The Amateur Softball Association (1351 Skirvin Tower, Oklahoma City, Okla. 73102) inaugurated its Youth Program in 1956, and it now provides supervised competition for more than 300,000 youngsters annually. Teams are organized according to age groups—nine to twelve, thirteen to fifteen, and sixteen to eighteen—although communities are permitted to formulate other age groups to suit local requirements.

Teams participating in the program receive ASA charter certificates, and individual players get membership cards and shoulder patches. The ASA also provides player record forms, rulebooks, instruction booklets on coaching and playing and literature on organization and administration.

Interestingly, the ASA discourages competition for young players on a regional or national basis, limiting tournaments to local or city levels. Only youngsters in the sixteen-to-eighteen-year-old bracket are permitted to compete on a statewide basis. "Younger children," says an ASA spokesman, "aren't emotionally prepared for competing beyond the state level."

Chicago, Dallas and Kansas City are among the cities that have flourishing junior softball programs. Active statewide programs are conducted in Oklahoma, Ohio, Texas, Alabama, Kansas, Minnesota and California, at least southern California.

These and all other junior programs operate autonomously through either a metropolitan or state association affiliated with the ASA. A commissioner is appointed to administer each association's program. If you wish to have your youngster or the team to which he belongs participate in the ASA's Youth Program, write to ASA headquarters and request the names of the metropolitan and state commissioners for your area.

BOOKS AND PUBLICATIONS

Novice players can benefit from *How to Improve Your Softball,* a 120-page instruction book containing close to 400 "how to" illustrations. Priced at 60¢, it's available from the Amateur Softball Association (see address above).

The ASA *Official Guide,* published annually in March, contains official fast- and slow-pitch rules, national tournament standings and statistical information. It costs 75¢.

ICE HOCKEY

About the only qualification one needs to play hockey is the ability to skate. It's a game that can be enjoyed by boys of all ages and every size. A sprinkling of girls also play the game. Seventeen-year-old Janet Goodman, the left wing for New York's Lehman College team, claims the most difficult part of the sport for her was waking up her father each morning when she was attending hockey instruction school. Her biggest problem with scrimmages is the stomach upsets she sometimes suffers before taking the ice.

Hockey is a fast game—indeed, it is often referred to as "the fastest game on earth"—and as such is an exhilarating one. About the only failing the sport has concerns facilities. You need ice, a frozen lake or an artificial rink. And even when facilities are available, they are often crowded.

Ice-hockey skating isn't quite the same as just plain recreational skating. The hockey player has to be much more skilled in starting with explosive speed and stopping abruptly. He has to be able to change direction quickly and to dart right or left in the blink of an eye. And all these skills have to be performed while he's puckhandling, awaiting a pass or seeking to avoid an opposing player.

Take a look at how professional players skate. They drive them-

251

selves forward with power-filled shoves, determinedly digging their blade edges into the ice on every stride. Their shoulders are slightly ahead of their hips, which helps them maintain their balance, even when being checked. Watch Bobby Orr, one of the best players, if not *the* best to enter pro ranks in recent years. He also happens to be one of the game's standout skaters, digging powerfully but smoothly on each stride.

If you happened to visit a training session for young players, you'd become immediately aware of another important aspect of hockey skating. "Keep your head up!" is what the coach is likely to be yelling constantly to his charges. Unless a player skates with his head high, he's not able to see where he's going or appraise what opposing players are going to do. And keeping erect also aids in breathing and maintaining a good supply of oxygen in the lungs. Canadian players, since they are schooled in techniques of hockey almost from the time they learn to walk, are well aware of the importance of keeping the head up. But American players, since they frequently learn how to skate first and play hockey later, aren't.

Hockey demands much greater stamina than most sports, and keeping in top physical condition is a year-round affair. Being in condition not only enables a boy to play his very best but is also a factor in helping to avoid injury.

Bicycling and running during the summer are recommended. Skipping rope is good because it helps develop the toe muscles, which are important to skating agility. Soccer, tennis and track and field are sports that dovetail nicely with hockey.

ICE-HOCKEY EQUIPMENT

The topic of selecting ice-hockey skates is covered in the chapter "Ice Skating." If your youngster is serious about the game, be sure he has his blades sharpened frequently. They should be ground in such a way that the blade is given both an inside and an outside edge. In other words, there will be a concave surface between the two blade edges. Blades should be resharpened after every four or five uses.

The blades should also be "rockered," which has to do with the amount of blade that is actually in contact with the ice. It varies with the individual and the position he plays. Check for rockering by putting the skate blades bottom-to-bottom and holding them out in front of you. Notice how the toe and heel areas curve away from each other; the blades touch only in the middle.

252

Ice Hockey

The skates that forwards wear should have more rockering than defensemen's skates. By reducing the amount of blade in contact with the ice, you increase the skate's maneuverability. By increasing the amount of blade on the ice, you increase the skater's stability and speed. Defensemen's skates should be rockered to give these characteristics.

To obtain the optimum in maneuverability, some professional players have their skates rockered to such a degree that only an inch or two of blade is in contact with the ice. Young players, however, need a much flatter blade, with at least four or five inches making contact.

Selecting a stick. Let the youngster choose his own hockey stick. It has to feel right for him.

The stick's lie is the first thing to be considered. This term refers to the angle which the handle makes with the blade. Manufacturers use a numbering system to identify lies. It usually ranges from 4 to 8, with a 4-lie stick indicating a very wide angle between the blade and shaft and higher numbers meaning a more acute angle.

The lie that's best for a young player depends to some extent on his skating style. If he bends from the waist as he skates, he'll probably need one of the lower-numbered lies. An upright skater needs a higher-number lie.

The stick's lie number will have some effect on the amount of power the boy is able to get into his shot. The lower the lie number, the more power. Higher-numbered lies, used by defensemen, contribute to shooting accuracy and one's ability to stickhandle. Generally, young players use a 5- or 6-lie stick. One way to determine whether a boy is using the right lie is to examine the blade of the stick after he's used it a few times. If it shows more wear at the heel than at the toe, he needs a lower lie. More wear at the toe indicates the opposite.

The length of the stick is also an important matter. Most coaches will tell you a stick is of the right length if, when held upright by the player in front of him (when he stands in street shoes), it reaches to his chin. Manufacturers make sticks in lengths appropriate for junior players, but if you can't seem to find one simply buy an adult model and saw off the end. This is a fairly common practice.

You also have to get a stick whose blade curves in the right direction. In this regard sticks can be right, left or neutral. A boy who shoots from the right side needs a "right" stick. A neutral stick has no curving, which enables the player to use both sides of the blade with equal facility when stickhandling. It also helps to keep shots low.

Several years ago, acutely curved sticks—banana blades, they're sometimes called—became popular. Coaches don't recommend sticks of this type for young players. The feeling is that they make puckhandling difficult—and they do. But young players see the professionals use them and are eager to imitate them.

About the only other factor to be considered is flexibility. The young player should test the stick to be sure that it's not too "whippy," yet it shouldn't be as stiff as a broom handle either. He has to arrive at a happy medium.

Once purchased, the stick has to be taped, even if it is glass-wrapped, as most newer models are. Black electrician's tape is traditional, but in recent years more and more players have been using white adhesive tape because it lasts longer. A single layer of tape, wound from the blade toe to the heel, aids in puck control.

Taping the top of the shaft helps the player to get a firmer grip. Some players wind several turns around the very end of the shaft to create a knob which helps to prevent the stick from being batted out of one's hands, and if it should be batted out the knobs aid in picking it up.

PROTECTIVE EQUIPMENT

In outfitting their youngsters for hockey and its hazards, many parents are guilty of buying too many items of equipment, often paying too much for them. The result, besides a deep dent in family finances, is that the youngster's mobility is restricted. It's all right to buy the very best when it's skates that you're purchasing, but with the balance of equipment the matter of quality is not always critical. And there are a few items that you can skip altogether.

A helmet is not one, however. It's vital. The helmet should be light in weight and comfortable, with a webbed suspension system that holds the outer shell well away from the wearer's head. Some helmets have mouthpieces attached which serve to protect the teeth, or you can buy a mouthpiece separately. If your youngster has difficulty breathing when using a mouthpiece or finds it otherwise uncomfortable, consult your family dentist. He can easily make the child a mouthpiece that fits perfectly. This type offers the greatest protection.

Elbow pads are also important. When a person falls, he frequently lands on his elbows. Padding them prevents cracked bones. The

Ice Hockey

youngster shouldn't go out onto the ice without them. The young player should wear shin pads, too. Made of tough shell plastic and held in place by the long stockings that players wear, they should protect not only the shin areas and the knee but the calf area of the leg as well.

Shoulder pads don't have to be big and cumbersome, at least for the very young player. In fact, they can take the form of shoulder caps, which attach to the suspenders. Teen-agers, however, do require a full shoulder harness which protects the collarbone area as well as the shoulders.

Gloves for young players don't have to be expensive. They should fully protect the back of the hand and thumb, but there is no necessity for them to reach to a point high on the forearm. Be sure the gloves fit snugly. Glove leather tends to stretch, and when the gloves are loose the player can't grip the stick firmly.

Hip pads can be built into the top of the hockey pants. The pants themselves should protect the lower back and be so adjusted that the bottom edge of the legs just covers the shin pads. Of course, the player has to wear a protective cup. Most players wear two-layer long underwear.

GOALTENDER'S EQUIPMENT

If your youngster is going to be tending goal on a regular basis, you'll want to outfit him with the specialized equipment the position demands. This includes goaltender's skates, ones which are not rockered in the slightest degree. The entire blade is flat to the ice—for obvious reasons. The blade is also a bit wider than the conventional blade, and the goaltender's boot is heavier and has added built-in protection.

The goalie's stick has a much higher lie number than the normal stick, usually as high as 14 or 15. This is because the stick has to be kept upright and flat to the ice most of the time.

Equipment for goalies is heavy and cumbersome, weighing as much as 30 pounds. There's no way to avoid this. Just do all that you can to be sure that the young player gets properly fitted.

This applies especially to face protection. A young and still-growing boy should wear a baseball-type wire mask, but an older boy should use a face-fitting mask of shell plastic. Have him try on several, checking not only for comfort and fit, but for vision, too. The mask should not obstruct his vision in any direction, up or down, right or left.

JUNIOR HOCKEY COMPETITION

There are many thousands of amateur hockey leagues active in the United States and Canada. They range from peewee and midget leagues for boys age six to eight, to senior leagues for adults. Junior hockey competition is often sponsored by city recreation departments, park boards, and community groups and service organizations. Of course, hundreds of high schools have hockey teams, and it's a thriving college sport in many areas.

Nonprofessional ice hockey is supervised by the Amateur Hockey Association of the United States (7901 Cedar Ave., Bloomington, Minn. 55420). About 100,000 amateur players belong to the organization. Besides its role in organizing leagues and arranging tournaments, the Association publishes a monthly bulletin and annual guidebook and a referee's manual.

INSTRUCTION BOOKS AND PUBLICATIONS

Just as the number of professional hockey teams has proliferated in recent years, so too has the number of instruction books. Most of the expansion teams varied in quality from mediocre to poor. The same

256

Ice Hockey

is true of the books. Better than the average, however, are *Inside Hockey* (Henry Regnery Company, $2.95), by Stan Makita, and *How to Play Hockey* (Doubleday, $4.95), by Tom Watts. The last-named not only covers the basics but has helpful diagrams illustrating offensive and defensive team play. Kids like these.

Many instruction books cover the goalie's chores in cursory fashion, but not *We Can Teach You to Play Hockey* (Hawthorn Books, $4.95), by Phil and Tony Esposito, both well-known pros. Tony, significantly, is the goaltender for the Chicago Black Hawks.

The rules of hockey are available at most stores that specialize in equipment. The National League rules, which are more or less followed by most young players, are available by writing league headquarters (922 Sun Life Building, Montreal, Quebec, Canada). They are also available in a paperback book titled *Ice Hockey Rules in Pictures* (Grosset & Dunlap, $1.85).

VOLLEYBALL

Volleyball, a vigorous game requiring quickness, speed and exacting skills, can be played indoors or out by boys and girls of all ages. The game has made rapid strides since 1964, the year it was introduced into Olympic competition.

Since the rules are simple and the *basic* skills not difficult to learn, almost any youngster can become fairly proficient in just an afternoon or two of practice, provided, of course, that he or she is not over-matched. But in high school competition, volleyball requires speed, agility and stamina. The conditioning program can be as rigorous as that for basketball or any other sport that requires constant running and charging. Knowledgeable coaches say it takes three seasons of competition for a high school athlete to develop into a top player.

A youngster is likely to be introduced to volleyball at a YMCA, community club or country club. In California, volleyball is a very popular beach sport. Although this version of the sport has no official recognition, organized competition is sponsored by city recreation departments and park departments. There are leagues and tournaments for six-man teams, six-woman teams, and mixed and doubles teams.

Many YMCAs have fully developed volleyball programs. This is

258

Volleyball

only logical because the game was invented in 1895 by one William G. Morgan, a student at Springfield College in Springfield, Massachusetts, and a director of the YMCA in nearby Holyoke. Morgan called the game Migonette at first, but as he experimented with the net and a ball, and the opposing teams kept "volleying" back and forth, he changed the name to volleyball. After an exhibition of the game at a physical directors' conference in Springfield, volleyball became popular almost everywhere. In 1897 the rules of volleyball were incorporated in the Handbook of the Athletic League of the YMCA of North America.

In 1928 the U.S. Volleyball Association (P.O. Box 554, Encino, Calif.) was founded. Today, through its seventeen regional divisions, the organization sanctions equipment, certifies officials, and sponsors regional and national tournaments. The USVBA also publishes an annual *Official Guide and Rule Book* and a quarterly magazine, *International Volleyball Review.*

EQUIPMENT

All the specialized equipment two teams require to play volleyball costs no more than a pair of ski boots. The major item is the ball itself. A top-quality indoor ball, white rubber with a nylon cover, is priced at about $12. For outdoor play on asphalt, a more durable outer covering is required. Players wear tennis shoes, shorts and loose-fitting shirts.

The volleyball court is 30 feet wide and 60 feet long. It is bounded by 2-inch-wide lines and divided by a center line, also 2 inches wide.

The net is 3 feet wide and stretched tautly above the center line. For men's play, the top edge of the net is 8 feet above the court surface. For women's play, the net is lowered to 7 feet 6 inches, and for juniors to 7 feet.

PLAY OF THE GAME

There are six players on a team, three stationed in the front half of the court and three in the rear half. The player in the right-rear position serves the ball. With every serve, the players on the serving team rotate clockwise, which gives each team member a serving opportunity.

The server, standing just behind the end line, throws the ball in the air and hits it with his hand, arm or fist, sending the ball over the net into the opponent's court. Once the serve is executed, the server steps back into the court.

The object of the game is for one team to attempt to score by grounding the ball on the opposing team's side of the net. A team is allowed a maximum of three touches per side before sending the ball across the net. A player is not permitted to hit the ball twice in succession except in the case of a simultaneous touch.

The usual strategy is for one player to tap the ball to a teammate, who then ''sets up'' the ball for a third teammate stationed close to the net. The third player leaps and smashes the ball—spikes it—into the opponent's court.

A game consists of 15 points but must be won by a 2-point margin. In tournament competition, games are sometimes played under a time limit, either eight or ten minutes to a game, with the team that accrues the most points winning. But this system encourages a team that is leading to use stalling tactics, and hence is not preferred.

INSTRUCTIONAL LITERATURE

Volleyball instruction books are few in number. However, *Sports Illustrated* recently added one to its library of sports-instruction titles. Called simply *Volleyball* (J. B. Lippincott, $3.95), it clearly and concisely explains such skills as the serve, the chest pass, the dig or save, the spike, the block, etc. It also gives the game's official rules.

GYMNASTICS

Gymnastics, like diving or figure skating, is a sport in which the individual performs both prescribed and optional exercises. Judges rate each performer on a point scale in tenths; 10.0 is perfect.

Don't confuse the gymnast with the acrobat. The acrobat must make even easy tricks look difficult. That's his stock in trade. The gymnast must appear effortless when performing the most complex routines.

Gymnastics provides a long list of values. It helps to develop the upper body—the shoulder girdle, triceps, abdomen and back—quicker and more effectively than almost any other activity you can name. And the muscles it builds are flexible and elastic.

The twisting, turning, bending and swinging movements the activity includes provide for the development of muscular coordination and what physical-fitness specialists call neuromuscular control. Things like fast forward rolls, hip circles on the horizontal bars or scissors on the trampoline develop a youngster's balance and poise, timing and sense of rhythm. During World War II, gymnastics was an essential feature of the physical-fitness program given to Navy pilots because the activity was known to develop courage and daring.

Physically, the gymnast is usually short and strong. He or she must

261

Gymnastics

have Spartan dedication, the will to be a twelve-month athlete. Daily preparation for school competition usually begins in September and continues into the spring. Coaches often assign their gymnasts to lift weights and do isometric exercises in the summer. Swimming, handball and tennis are often recommended. The training program has to include components that provide not only for strength and stamina, but for agility, flexibility and balance as well.

With proper supervision, a youngster can begin gymnastics training at a very early age. Boys and girls of five or six can be taught to execute forward and backward rolls and head stands. The Tumbling Tots, a citywide gymnastics program that is active in Tallahassee, Florida, features youngsters of from seven to fifteen. Their presentations include tumbling, balancing, juggling and trampoline work.

SAFETY

Parents often regard gymnastics as being a hazardous activity, but statistics demonstrate that injuries are few. Some precautions are necessary, however. The gymnast has to warm up sufficiently; he has to stretch his muscles and loosen his joints before attempting the simplest stunt. Coaches agree that such preparation is a vital factor in the prevention of injuries.

The gymnast should make a habit of inspecting the apparatus before the training session begins to be certain that adjustments are secure. The apparatus should be so positioned so that it is clear of obstructions. Mats should be checked, too; they must provide sufficient padding and they must be level.

One's attitude is important. When attempting a new trick, the gymnast must make a total commitment to its completion. Indecision is as hazardous as slippery fingers.

The gymnast should never work alone; he should always have a spotter. There is nothing new about working out under a spotter's supervision, but in recent years the role of the spotter has changed. It used to be that the spotter would attempt to prevent an injury *after* the performer had fallen. But the idea today is for the spotter to ensure that the gymnast successfully completes each stunt he attempts. Thus, falls are prevented. The spotter does this by supplying any force or motion that the performer fails to provide.

Of course, this means that the spotter has to know the mechanics of each trick, and know them at least as well as the performer. He also has to be able to anticipate the performer's movement, putting his hands on him *before* the moment of need. Skilled spotting not only prevents serious injury but also helps to build the performer's confidence.

COMPETITION

The AAU supervises gymnastics competition. Boys and girls compete separately in age-group divisions.

The major events for boys include the horizontal bar, parallel bars, side horse, long horse (also called the vaulting horse), stationary rings, floor exercises (calisthenics), and all-around, an event that combines all of the other six.

Girls' events are the balance beam, uneven parallel bars, vaulting horse, floor exercises (like the boys', but set to music), and all-around.

Each category includes both compulsory and optional stunts. The former are graded on the basis of form, ease of execution, grace, rhythm, balance, timing and perfection in the performance of each

Gymnastics

individual part. Optional exercises are rated on the basis of originality, difficulty, artistic grace and the performer's skill in blending together the individual parts of each trick.

For more information, write to the AAU (3400 West 86th St., Indianapolis, Ind. 46268) and request a copy of the *Gymnastics Handbook,* which costs $2.50. It gives the rules and equipment specifications for junior competition.

TRACK
AND
FIELD

Techniques and training methods in track and field have undergone many significant changes in recent years, and enormous progress has been the result, progress that can be measured by the great number of records that fall each year. And while this means it is becoming ever more difficult to become a champion performer, no one is saying that future progress is not possible. It simply means trying harder.

The United States has held a leadership position in track and field for many years, thanks to our high schools and colleges, which provide training and competition that is, according to *A World History of Track and Field Athletics,* by Roberto Quercetani, ''unquestionably the stiffest in the world.''

It was true a generation ago and it is true today—speed, stamina and strength are the qualities that a boy or girl requires to be successful in track and field. A runner's speed relates to the rate and length of his stride. It is also linked to skills he can sharpen through training, such as learning how to start explosively or how to take a hurdle.

Strength provides power and thrust. Stamina refers to endurance, both muscular endurance and the overall ability of the body to perform a strenuous activity for a sustained period.

In addition to speed, stamina and strength, there are psychological

266

Track and Field

aspects to track and field—such factors as determination, the ability to resist pain and fatigue, skill in planning training sessions and judging pace, confidence, and the ability to perform under pressure.

As one coach expresses it, "Training only makes successful running possible. The runner himself, his competitive instinct, must transform the potential into reality."

The training program for most runners requires at least an hour a day, five days a week, and virtually twelve months a year. What the training program consists of depends on the type of running the athlete does (see categories below) and the particular training theories to which his coach subscribes. There are many opinions as to what is best, but the program is certain to include plenty of running. A hundred or more miles a week is not unusual. As the young runner becomes more proficient, the training load is increased in both amount and intensity.

Some coaches stress weight training in addition to running, and encourage their athletes to spend at least an hour or so a week lifting weights. Lifting heavy weights a relatively few times builds strength. Lifting light weights many times builds endurance.

Training is something your youngster should be diligent about. But his schedule should not impose real hardship or subject him to drudgery.

EQUIPMENT

Track and field require little in the way of equipment—just a pair of sneakers for warming up and two pairs of spiked shoes (one for workouts and one for competition), plus tee shirts, running shorts, socks and sweat suit.

TRACK EVENTS

The AAU (3400 West 86th St., Indianapolis, Ind. 46268) is the ruling body for track and field in the United States. It conducts regional and national championships and a junior olympics program as well. Rules and records for the various track and field events are contained in the AAU's *Track and Field Handbook*. It costs $3.00.

In both track and field, men compete against men, women against women. Track events can be grouped into these categories:

Sprints. These are races up to and including the 220-yard dash. For younger children, there are also the 50- and 75-yard dashes. The runner starts from a crouch, his feet braced against starting blocks.

What physical qualities does a youngster need in order to be a successful sprinter? Speed in muscular contraction is surely one. How fast can he work his muscles? If he can move at the rate of four and a half steps per second, then he can become a topflight sprinter. Other important factors are the length of his stride, his reaction time, endurance and overall flexibility.

Middle distances.   Races of 440 yards, 880 yards and one mile are known as middle-distance events. The start is from a crouch or standing position.

As the distance of the races increases, the importance of speed and strength begin to diminish, while the need for stamina increases sharply. Successful middle-distance runners can be of almost any physical type, tall or short, slim or husky.

Long distances.   These are races of more than a mile's distance. Only boys and girls age fourteen and older compete in long-distance races, and seldom is any event longer than 3 miles.

Hurdles.   The hurdles are usually run by boys and girls who excel in sprints. Besides the gift of speed, these events require agility and balance.

Many young people have a misconception about hurdling. They think it means jumping, which it does not; the hurdler simply sprints over the barriers.

Hurdling competition for boys begins at age fourteen with the 70-yard high (39-inch) hurdles, 120-yard high hurdles and 120-yard low (30-inch) hurdles. For fourteen-year-old girls, there is the 80-yard low hurdles.

Boys of sixteen and seventeen often compete in the 220-yard intermediate (36-inch) hurdles, the 180-yard low hurdles and the 120-yard high hurdles. Girls of sixteen and seventeen compete in the 80-yard low hurdles.

Race walking.   Boys (not girls) of eight and nine often compete in walking races of 660 or 880 yards, and for older boys, age sixteen and seventeen, there are walking races of 1, 3, and 6 miles. In walking competition, the rule is that the advancing foot must contact the ground before the rear foot leaves the ground. During each step, the forward knee must be momentarily straight and the body erect.

FIELD EVENTS

Field events are concerned with jumping and throwing things. For young children, however, competition involves only the former. Not until a boy or girl is ten or eleven is he or she deemed ready for throwing competition, and then it's only a lightweight—6-pound—shot.

Youngsters begin competition in the pole vault at twelve or thirteen. At fourteen or fifteen, boys are introduced to the discus and 12-pound shot. Only older boys, those sixteen and seventeen, and girls, too, compete in javelin competition.

Youngsters of every age enjoy the high jump, and are able to clear the bar at levels well above their height. Generally, the better high jumpers are tall and slender. But what really counts are an explosive takeoff and the ability to "roll" over the bar.

The running broad jump is also popular, especially among boys and girls who perform well as sprinters. The speed they gather as they streak down the runway gives them momentum for the leap.

PHOTOGRAPH CREDITS

10, Princeton Community Tennis Program; 11, 12, U.S. Lawn Tennis Association; 17, 18, 24, 25, Wagner International Photos, Inc.; 36, George Sullivan; 37, 39, Wake Forest University; 40, Dom Lupo; 41, University of Houston; 46, Shakespeare, Sporting Goods Division; 50, Squaw Valley, Calif.; 51, Winter Park, Colo.; 57, George Sullivan; 60, Wagner International Photos, Inc.; 62, 64, George Sullivan; 69, Amateur Fencers League of America (John Nicolas); 72, 75, AMF; 79, 81, 82, Wagner International Photos, Inc.; 91, Girl Scouts of the USA; 94, 95, 96, Wagner International Photos, Inc.; 103, Bahama News Bureau; 105, George Sullivan; 106, 107, Bahama News Bureau; 113, 114, 115, American Water Ski Association; 127, 136, 138, Winchester-Western; 147, 148, Evinrude; 152, O'Day Corp.; 153, State of Florida; 154, Alpex; 157, 158, St. Francis Preparatory School, Brooklyn, N.Y.; 168, Bass Boots, Inc.; 171, U.S. Dept. of Interior, National Park Service (Fred Mang); 172, USDA Forest Service (Jim Hughes); 179, Evinrude; 186, Bicycle Institute of America, Inc.; 191, American Youth Hostels (Ted Kinman); 198, Princeton University; 199, Yale University; 204, Wagner International Photos, Inc.; 208, Au Tatso Judo Club, El Paso, Texas; 210, U.S. Judo Federation; 224, 226, 231, 233, 237, George Sullivan; 238, Wagner International Photos, Inc., 242, 243, George Sullivan; 248, Amateur Softball Association; 255, Riverdale Rink; 260, George Sullivan; 262, Pennsylvania State University; 264, U.S. Naval Academy; 267, 268, Wagner International Photos, Inc.; 271, George Sullivan.